The Essential Guide to Running for Local Office

How to Plan, Organize and Win Your Next Election

Paul F. Caranci

The Essential Guide to Running for Local Office

How to Plan, Organize and Win Your Next Election

By

Paul F. Caranci

The Essential Guide to Running for Local Office: How to Plan, Organize and Win Your Next Election Copyright © 2014 Paul F. Caranci. Produced and printed by Stillwater River Publications. All rights reserved. Written and produced in the United States of America. This book may not be reproduced or sold in any form without the expressed, written permission of the author and publisher.

Visit our website **at www.StillwaterPress.com** for more information.

First Stillwater River Publications Edition
ISBN-10: 0-692-24202-3
ISBN-13 978-069224-202-5

Library of Congress Control Number: 201494373

1 2 3 4 5 6 7 8 9 10
Written by Paul F. Caranci
Cover design by Dawn M. Porter
Published by Stillwater River Publications, Glocester, RI, USA

Table of Contents

Disclaimer

The information in this book is intended to be a general guide to assist a candidate running for a local elected office. Be aware, however, that laws governing candidates and their activities often vary from state to state and from political jurisdiction to political jurisdiction. Campaign finance laws, reporting requirements, filing deadlines, polling place activities, etc. are also specific to the office being sought and the region in which you will be a candidate. Even activities as seemingly mundane as the placement of lawn signs or the location of a campaign headquarters are subject to local zoning laws and other rules and regulations. Be sure to check with the appropriate state and local officials within your state and political jurisdiction to identify and verify the applicable laws, rules and regulations for candidates and campaign activities in your area. It is always advisable to consult with a local attorney that is familiar with election laws and requirements to verify the specific requirements of your local jurisdiction.

Dedication

During the more than sixteen years that I held elective office on the North Providence town council, the eight years prior that I served as an a appointed member of the Town's zoning board and the nearly forty-five years of my life that was consumed by politics, I had the pleasure of meeting some extraordinary people. Their support and friendship, in many ways, changed my life. I am grateful to all of them, but in particular express my continued gratitude to my closest friends and supporters; Frank Anzeveno and Arthur, "Doc" Corvese, two of the most dedicated public servants to enter the profession, my attorney, Fred Marzilli, who stands among the most equitable jurists to ever serve on the bench, Jim "the fly" Walker whose dedication and constant source of information, regardless of where in the world he happened to be when that information was needed proved invaluable and Bob Cerilli and his wife Jo-Anne who did everything from manage my campaigns to procure more sign locations than any one candidate deserves. Also, the two women, Donna M. Melikian and Lynne Murphy Hickey, who served at various times as my campaign manager each bringing to my election efforts qualities of loyalty, hard work, dedication, support and above all, the friendship that was so critical to my unbroken string of electoral victories. Each of these people afforded me the opportunity to do what I love for so many years – work to improve the quality of life for those that I was elected to serve.

My decision to dedicate a large portion of my life to public service, however, could not have been possible without the love, sacrifice and constant unwavering support of my family. To them I owe everything; my parents Frank and Anne, who despite my undeserving nature, and their failing health, dropped whatever else they may have been doing to support my many campaigns; my sister Linda, brother-in-law Dennis and nephew Michael Corsini, who served on more committees and dedicated more time to activities that they really didn't enjoy simply to help advance my efforts; my children Heather and Matthew who, as small children understood when hundreds of hours of campaigning, or an ill-timed meeting, caused me to miss more than one ball game or family dinner, and who as young adults did so much of the "grunt" work required in a campaign; my mother-in-law, Carol LaCourse who did whatever was needed of her; my Aunt Rita McCaughey who always helped with my fundraisers; and my wife, best friend and most ardent supporter, Margie, who sacrificed the most and seldom complained even when forced to spend our 18th wedding anniversary attending a 1995 D.A.R.E graduation at which I was the principal speaker, followed by a spaghetti dinner held in my honor at one of the local senior citizen housing complexes.

I hope God holds a special place for them all. I'm certain that I do.

This book is dedicated to all of them.

Preface

There are well over 500,000 elected officials in the United States. That number may easily swell to over 5 million worldwide. The positions to which those local officials are elected encompass all three branches of government - executive, legislative and judicial. They include municipal offices such as mayor, school board and council. They also include positions in the nation's state legislatures. Some jurisdictions even hold elections to fill positions such as town clerk, sheriff and municipal judge.

Regardless of jurisdiction and position, all of those elected are required to swear an oath of office to uphold the constitution of the United States as well as their state constitution, the municipal charter and any other laws enforced within the jurisdiction they were elected to represent.

While the duties and terms of their respective offices can vary widely, they all have one thing in common. Each of them competed for a local office and won. Yet, for everyone that was successfully elected to a local office, there were many more candidates that were not. In many cases the only thing that separated the winners from the losers was the specific knowledge of how to run for a local elected office. Running for a local office requires a specific skill set not necessarily utilized by candidates for higher office. The reason is because a local election allows for a much more personal and intimate interaction with the voters than a statewide or federal election does.

This book will provide you with a basic understanding of what it takes to compete as a candidate for a local office. More than a guide this book provides a blueprint for running for a local elected office in the United States. If there is one certainty in politics it is that there is no way of knowing what moves the electorate to vote a particular way. Yet, there are certain steps that should be executed in the electoral process that, when taken, can move a candidate toward victory.

Election laws vary widely from state to state and then again within the various political subdivisions within each state. It is critical, therefore, that the advice and suggestions enumerated within the pages of this book be carefully checked against the laws of the jurisdiction within which you are a candidate. Naturally, it is always best to consult an attorney whenever you are interpreting your jurisdictional laws and running for office is certainly no exception to that rule.

Following the recommendations in this book will make for an efficient and effective campaign, one certainly capable of enabling the candidate to win the election bringing you one step closer to the victory that you so eagerly seek. Good luck to you as you toss your own hat into the proverbial ring.

Section I
The Decision to Run or Not to Run

Running for public elective office is a major commitment that should not be taken lightly. Effective campaigning can be both time consuming and very expensive. It may have implications on many other people. Your family and friends could become fair game for opponent criticism and press coverage. Your private and quiet life as you know it could be over and you and your family members may have to grow accustomed to living life in a bubble. The time commitment of both campaigning for, and serving in, a public office may have a detrimental impact on your social life and the financial burden may leave you wishing you had taken on a second job at McDonald's instead of financing the campaign.

 On the other hand, running for public office offers significant benefits as well. You will certainly meet your neighbors. You will make new friends, develop long lasting relationships with those who so enthusiastically support your effort, and have a chance to bring awareness to many issues that you hold dear. You may learn new skills, become a better public speaker and gain confidence in yourself.

Winning provides even more personal satisfaction as you will have the opportunity to help people in need and improve the quality of life for everyone.

Despite the potential drawbacks and/or benefits of seeking local public office, a decision to become a candidate should be given a significant amount of thought and should not be made in a vacuum. Discuss it with your spouse, significant other, family members and close friends. You will need their support if you are to campaign effectively. The next few chapters will address the issues that you will want to consider and discuss before making your decision to begin a campaign.

Chapter 1
A Reason to Run for Public Office

People decide to run for office for any number of reasons. Some are driven by a desire to serve the public. Others want to give back to a community that has so wonderfully enriched their lives. Still others are recruited by another person or organization looking to execute an agenda while some are simply passionate about a particular issue. There are even those who run for public office simply to challenge and hopefully replace an official that might not be working in the best interest of the community.

NOTE: If there is a significant amount of external pressure being applied on you to run for office, then you might want to abandon your campaign before you go any further! Running for office is a major commitment, one you should undertake only if you are willing to put your whole heart and soul into the race.

Whatever your motivation, you must first decide if seeking public office is the best way to achieve the objective. Of course, it is always better if you are running for a positive reason, IE to help the community, rather than a negative one, IE as payback for not getting something from a public official that you may have wanted. Only you will know your true motivation for seeking election to public office. Regardless of the reason, you will need to analyze your true motivation in order to adequately respond to a question that you will more than likely be asked – Why do you want to be a councilman or school board member?

It's been said that some people run for office to be something and some run for office to accomplish something. The title or the potential personal benefits should never be your sole motivation to seek elective office. You should always derive your motivation from the prospect of helping others and/or improving your community. If you are sincere about running for those altruistic reasons, not only will the voters sense your sincerity, but you will be well on your way to becoming a productive, ethical and honest politician.

Finally, be prepared to un-hesitantly answer the inevitable question when asked, "Why do you want to run for office?" I remember a reporter asking Ted Kennedy during a television interview in his 1980 campaign for president why he wanted to run. Kennedy stumbled, stammered, hesitated and eventually offered a feeble answer at best. That response defined his short and fledgling campaign and led to its eventual demise.

Chapter 2
Meeting the Criteria for Public Office

Answering the question "why?" is only the first step in deciding whether or not you should run for office. There are many procedural issues you must also address, some of which could have a negative impact on your ability to become a candidate for public office.

First, you must be a qualified elector. That is, a registered voter who has reached the age requirement for the office you seek. In most jurisdictions you must be at least 18 years of age to vote and therefore to be a candidate for office. Many jurisdictions, however, impose additional requirements. For example, you may need to be registered to vote a certain number of days prior to the filing or declaration period, *(Declarations of candidacy are discussed in greater detail in section II of this book)* and the local town charter may require a candidate for certain offices such a mayor for example, to reach a more advanced age than the age required to run for other offices. Further, there may be a requirement that you live in the district in which you are running for a period of time prior to running for, or serving in, the position. There could be a host of other requirements as well.

 If you are not sure whether or not you are registered to vote from your current address, you should contact the board of canvassers of your local city or town. The clerk will be able to tell you in a matter of minutes if you are registered, from what address you are registered, and how long you have been registered there. The clerk may also be able to provide your entire voting history including your party designation. Voters may be registered as an independent or with a party affiliation such as Democrat, Republican or other recognized party. In many jurisdictions, a registered Democrat may not be eligible to run as a Republican, and vice versa, without first joining that party. Once again, the clerk of the local board of canvassers can provide that information and provide the voter registration card with which to change your party affiliation if need be.

In terms of age, residency or any other potential requirement, you should consult your town charter and/or review your state laws. Never simply rely on another's opinion even if that someone works for your municipal or state government unless you get the information in writing with citations informing you of the source of the requirement allowing you the opportunity to check the information yourself. Clerks can make a mistake or give information that is technically correct, but not responsive to your exact question. A hasty or wrong answer can create significant issues for you later on.

Regardless of your information source, it is always best to verify the information you get with a second source. In many states the Secretary of State's Office or a statewide elections board may be a good source of verification of this type of information. An hour of time invested at this stage of the campaign can save you a lot of headaches and heartaches farther down the road. Take the time to verify the information you receive!

Chapter 3
Choosing the Right Office to Seek

As stated earlier, there are a plethora of choices when it comes to running for a local elected office. The position you run for really depends on your specific interests. For example if you are interested in seeking office because you want your local school department to offer a full-time kindergarten option or because you want to expand the number of charter schools available in your area, then the school board might be your best choice of position. However, if you are running because you want to reduce taxes or expand public services, you may choose to run for the office of town council or mayor.

Another consideration in selecting the position for which you run is the cost of running for office. More than likely the lower the "importance" of the position, or the smaller the district in which you will have to compete, the less expensive your campaign will be. Running for a town-wide office for example, will be far more expensive than running in a district that comprises only 1/3 of the town.

The mayor or town administrator generally is elected town-wide. Council and school committee seats can be district-wide or town-wide. The council and school committee seats that are elected on a town-wide basis are generally referred to as At-Large positions.

A further consideration is whether or not the seat is "open," meaning that the incumbent (the person currently occupying the position) will not be seeking re-election. Clearly, unless an incumbent has done something terribly wrong or has done little or nothing to serve the voter's needs, it is less expensive to run, and easier to win, a position in which the incumbent will not be running. In many areas of the country, it is difficult to beat a candidate that has held an office for a long time because he/she has probably helped a great many people over the years; people who now feel they owe the incumbent a vote of support and allegiance. The exception, of course, is the case of a long-time office holder who has wronged the town's people or has been caught up in some sort of scandal. Those incumbents may be vulnerable despite their extensive time in office.

Chapter 4
Factors That Might Influence
Your Decision to be a Candidate

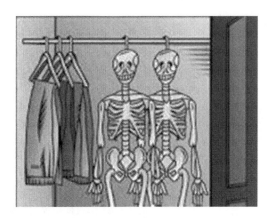

When it comes to running for and holding an elective office you do not necessarily hold all the decision-making cards in your own hands! Your decision, as was stated earlier, will affect many other people and their feelings should be considered as well. Among the several influences that must be factored into your final decision are the impact to your family, your employers and your wallet.

Politics can be a brutal, unforgiving pastime. An opponent may stop at nothing to defeat you and many times unsuspecting family members can become ensnared in the political fray. If you, a spouse, child, parent or sibling have a past indiscretion, it very likely could be exposed during the campaign. The press may question you or a family member about it and your formerly personal issue may become a front page headline of your local newspaper or fodder for the day's, maybe even the week's, radio talk shows. In fact, the "indiscretion" doesn't even have to be an illegal activity. Something as perfectly legal as a prior bankruptcy proceeding can be used by an opponent to attempt to show that you may be unfit to care for the town's purse. Unfair as this may seem, you should have a very frank discussion with everyone involved before making your decision. Discuss with them some of those issues and the potential for the formerly private issue to be vetted in a public forum.

You and your family will need to have, or grow, a very thick skin to survive life under the proverbial microscope. While this may not seem fair, it is the reality of politics in many jurisdictions throughout the country. It is better to be prepared early on than to be caught off guard and embarrassed publicly only to have your campaign derailed later as a result.

Another family consideration is the age of your children, parents and/or others whose care may be your responsibility. Are your children young, involved in local sports leagues, having problems academically or otherwise placing demands on your time beyond that normally required of a parent? Are your parents elderly or physically ill and dependent on your daily or nightly care? Campaigning for public office will place demands on your time that may adversely impact your ability to be there for your family members. Your decision to run for office should certainly take all of these considerations into account.

In addition to family considerations, your job may impose obstacles to your ability to effectively campaign for office. For example, if any part of your income is derived from federal funds, you may be prohibited under provisions of the federal Hatch Act from raising funds or campaigning for a partisan office. If you are uncertain if the Hatch Act applies to you, you may seek a written advisory opinion by writing to The United States Department of Justice, Office of Special Counsel, 1730 M Street, N.W., Suite 218, Washington, D.C. 20036-4505. You may also contact them by telephone at 202-254-3600. I believe it is always advisable to have written copies of such correspondence even though that may delay the process a bit.

Depending upon the position that you hold in your job, there may be state or local laws that might also impede your ability to seek public office. For example, some jurisdictions have either state laws or municipal charter provisions that prevent town employees from seeking office within a town in which they are employed. Some states prohibit state employees from holding positions in the state legislature. However, while such prohibitions may be in place, there may also be exemptions from the restrictions that could apply to you. Firemen and educators, for example, are sometimes exempted from the prohibition against holding office in the municipality in which they are employed. Be sure to read through the entire state law or charter provision to ensure that your specific employment is in fact subject to a restriction and seek appropriate legal advice when necessary.

Another practical job consideration may be the hours that you are required to work. For example, meetings of many municipal boards, commissions and councils are generally held in the evening. If you work a third shift job, you may be unable to attend the meetings of the council position for which you are a candidate. Similarly, many part-time state legislatures meet during the late afternoon and into the early evening. Be sure to check the demands of the elected position prior to making a commitment that you might not be able to keep should you win.

Even if you are able to attend the meetings of the board for which you are a candidate and meet all the legal requirements, your boss may not want you to become involved in local politics. Perhaps you work for a public relations firm that represents candidates of various political parties and philosophies and the firm has a policy regarding political neutrality that your candidacy may violate. It is always better to clear the idea of running with the boss first rather than to raise and spend campaign money, announce your candidacy, and then be informed by your boss that you cannot keep your job and be a candidate for public office.

Financial considerations should also be taken into account. Be sure that you will be able to financially afford the commitment you are about to make. How much will your campaign cost? How will you raise the revenue necessary to both campaign and hold office? Will campaigning and holding office require that you relinquish that part time job that helped you pay your mortgage? Even if the potential compensation from the position offsets the income you may have to sacrifice, what will happen if you give up your part time job and fail to win the election? Will you then be able to get your job back or get another job that can match the compensation from the one you lost? While you certainly may not want to enter into a campaign thinking about the prospect of not winning, that option is one you may need to consider for the sake of your financial well - being.

Finally, consider whether you hold a certain stature within your community that may aid you in your campaign efforts. Historically there are many successful candidates that never had prior involvement with their community. However, those who have a history of involvement with church groups or social community organizations such as the Lions or Rotary Clubs, or community sports groups such as the Little League or the local youth basketball, football or soccer leagues, may already have a significant base of support that can be tapped for the campaign. All else being equal such support, which often translates into votes, volunteers and financial contributions, may be hard for a challenger to overcome and may play a major role in your final decision to run.

Making a decision to run for a local elective office will very often require you to consider many factors that may, at first blush, not seem relevant to your decision. Be assured that they *are* relevant and you will need to give them proper weight and well-thought out reflection before reaching a decision to run for office. Don't take these issues lightly. If you and your family do some careful soul searching before making an affirmative decision to initiate a campaign, you will position yourself better and become a much more effective campaigner as a result.

Section II
The Planning Stage
Planning the Work

Chapter 5
Administrative
and Procedural Responsibilities

The Declaration Process

Most states establish a period of time preceding each election cycle in which those wanting to run for an elective office must "declare" their candidacies. These "declaration periods," can take place 90 or 120 days prior to the primary election and usually signal the "official" start of the campaign season. Each prospective candidate is generally required to sign a declaration enumerating the position to which the candidate aspires and the party he/she intends to represent. For example, a Republican candidate for a town council seat will be required to sign a prescribed form indicating his intention to enter the primary of the Republican Party as a candidate for the town council. (A

Sample Declaration Form is included in the Appendix on page 189.)

Declaration forms for local offices are typically filed with the municipal board of canvassers while those declaring for a state office may be required to file with the Secretary of State or the State Elections Board. The place, time and format for filing declarations of candidacy may vary widely from state to state or even from county to county so it is vitally important to check with your local or state board early to determine where, when and exactly what you need to file. One thing is certain, however. If you fail to adhere to the declaration period filing requirement you typically will not be allowed to run for elective office in that election cycle.

The Nomination Process

Every candidate who files a declaration will be notified of another potential requirement - the need to collect signatures on an official set of nomination papers. Not all jurisdictions require the collection of signatures in order to run for local office and those that do may require varying numbers of qualified signatures depending on the office being sought. For example, a person running for mayor may need to collect 200 qualified signatures while a candidate for a district council seat may need to collect only 50. Once again, it is important that you determine the exact number of signatures needed for the particular office you intend to seek.

Some candidates make the critical mistake of collecting only the number of signatures actually needed to qualify as a candidate for the office to which they aspire. Making this mistake can prove fatal to your candidacy. Officials from your local elections board will review each signature that you collect and compare it to the voter registration list. If the person who signed your nomination paper is not a "qualified" elector, that signature will be disqualified. Even if the signer is a registered voter, he/she may not be registered from the district in which you are running and consequently that signature will not be counted toward the qualifying names on your nominations papers. If you fail to submit the correct number of signatures from "qualified" electors, your candidacy will be disqualified.

It is always a good practice to gather and submit as many signatures as possible. Doing this will accomplish two objectives; first, it dramatically improves the chances that you will qualify for ballot placement, and second, it will provide you a base of names of qualified electors who, if not yet supporters of your efforts, have at least indicated that they have no objection to your candidacy. These people are a good source of support for you and with the proper cultivation may easily be turned into supporters.

Take advantage of the opportunity to send each person who signed your papers a thank you letter. Enclose a brochure or flyer explaining your platform and asking them for their support. Mail a separate letter to each individual, not a single letter addressed to the entire family. That way, everybody that signed your papers will be sure to receive the letter. Frequently, local elections are about name recognition. The more times a voter is exposed to your name, the greater the likelihood that he/she will remember your name on election day.

While many look at the nomination process as one giant pain in the butt, I have always viewed it as a golden opportunity to confirm and expand my base of support.

Campaign Finance Reporting

Another critically important administrative requirement is that of campaign finance reporting. These reports are normally filed with the state board of elections or your particular state's equivalent. This filing process can actually encompass the filing of several reports and generally have the force of law behind them. They are to be taken seriously and compliance should never be ignored. Depending on the state, political jurisdiction, and local office sought, such forms may include, but not be limited to the following:

❖ The *Notice of Organization* form generally allows you to designate a campaign treasurer. The treasurer has an awesome responsibility in the campaign. That person must accept, process and deposit all campaign donations, and compile a record of information for each donor. It is the responsibility of the treasurer and ultimately the candidate to ensure that not one prohibited contribution is accepted.

➤ A prohibited or illegal contribution is one that is prohibited by the federal or state constitutions and laws as well as any federal, state or local rules and regulations. Many states, for example, prohibit candidates from accepting a cash donation (or limit the amount of cash that can be donated by a single donor). Likewise, many states prohibit a candidate from accepting corporate or business contributions.

➤ The treasurer will generally assume the responsibility of ensuring compliance with all campaign finance laws, rules and regulations on behalf of the candidate. This person must be someone that you trust completely with your money and your reputation.

NOTE: Campaign finance laws have been in recent years, and may continue to be in future years, the subject of review by the United States Supreme Court on the basis of 1st Amendment free speech rights. It is important, therefore, to check with your state and/or local boards or your campaign attorney for the most current information available at the time of your candidacy.

➢ Frequently, the same contributor will make more than one donation to your campaign during the same election cycle. A record must be kept of each contribution made by every individual so that you will know when that person has reached the limit of allowable aggregate contributions in each election cycle as established by law in your state or political jurisdiction. Many states, after all, do have laws limiting the aggregate contribution from any one individual or political action committee (PAC).

➢ All of this information must be reported on a quarterly basis, or more frequently in the days just prior to and just following, the election. A filer who does not pay close attention to detail may inadvertently accept an "illegal" contribution thereby causing you a significant amount of adverse publicity and potential legal problems that could derail your campaign or worse!

➢ I always acted as my own treasurer or asked my wife to accept the responsibility for me. This certainly added an additional burden at a time when I could least afford to be stressed, but it also assured that the job was being handled correctly and I knew I would never have to attempt to explain why an inappropriate contribution was inadvertently accepted by my campaign. In some cases, it meant returning a sizable contribution made by a local businessman on a corporate check. Though I would always ask that the donor replace the contribution with a personal or PAC check, it did not always happen. At the end of the day, however, I could sleep well at night knowing that I was in full compliance with federal, state and local campaign finance law.

➢   In most states the candidate is allowed to act as his own treasurer, but before making that designation, get confirmation from your local elections board. The local election officials are generally very willing to answer any questions you have about compliance since they want to ensure as much compliance from as many candidates as possible. It is always advisable however to get any interpretations of legal requirements in writing so that you will have documentation for future reference should an issue arise.

❖   The *Summary of Campaign Finance* form is just that; a form that summarizes the total revenue and expenditures of the campaign during the specific reporting period. It reports the opening and closing balance of campaign cash and/or assets and liabilities, the period's revenues and expenses and any loans or outstanding invoices that the campaign has accumulated. The information listed on this page is generally gleaned from two other more detailed reports, namely;

❖   The *Schedule of Contributions Received* form requires you to list the name, address and occupation of each campaign donor as well as the date that the contribution was received and the contribution amount. This form will sometimes contain space for the reporting of 3 or 4 different donors per page. It may, and hopefully will, be several pages long.

❖ The *Schedule of Expenditures* form allows for the recording of each individual campaign expense and requires the reporting of the name and address of the payee or vendor, the date of payment and the amount. It too contains space to record several transactions per page and could require several pages.

❖ Some states allow for the filing of an *Affidavit for Annual Filing Exemption* form. This form allows the treasurer to sign an affidavit acknowledging that no contributions in excess of $100 in the aggregate from a single source and no aggregate expenditures in excess of $1,000 will occur within the calendar year. *NOTE: these amounts may vary in different political jurisdictions.*

❖ Finally, the *Affidavit Dissolving Campaign Account* form needs to be filed when you decide that you will no longer be a candidate for office and there is no money remaining in your account. At this time you will need to make a final accounting of the disbursement of any monies that remained in your account at the time of closing.

NOTE: the nomenclature of the aforementioned forms is that used in Rhode Island by the RI State Board of Elections. The forms in your state, though probably gathering similar if not identical information, may likely be identified by a different name.

❖ One more thing regarding campaign finance; it is generally accepted practice to open a bank account under a selected campaign name. For example you may choose to name your account "Friends of John Smith," or "John Smith for Council," or "John Smith 2016." Whichever campaign account name you select, you should ask that any contribution check be made out by the donor to that account name so that you will not have a problem depositing the checks.

➤ Some banks will allow you to open the account with your social security number, but it is advisable to obtain a separate federal employer ID number (FEIN) for the campaign from the IRS rather than to use your own social security number. Applying for an FEIN is a relatively easy process and can be done on-line at http://www.irs.gov/Businesses/Small-Businesses-&-Self-Employed/Apply-for-an-Employer-Identification-Number-(EIN)-Online.

➤ Once established, this account should be used to purchase all goods and pay any vendor. All deposits of political contributions or loans to your campaign fund throughout the entire campaign period (and beyond if you are successful or anticipate running again) should be made into this account as well.

NOTE: Never cash a check, always deposit them so that there is a complete record of all money received and all money spent.

✓ It is never a good idea, and may even be illegal in some jurisdictions, to co-mingle campaign funds with your personal or business funds.

NOTE: if you maintain your campaign account after the election in anticipation of running for office again in the future, you may need to continue to file quarterly campaign finance reports with your appropriate state or local elections board for the entire period that your account remains open, even if you are not a candidate for office in the particular year.

Most forms come with a complete set of instructions and are fairly straight forward but if you are confused by the instructions, don't hesitate to ask your local election board officials for assistance. Most are very happy to help you in order to ensure your compliance with the reporting requirements. (Sample Campaign Finance Forms are included in Appendix on pages 172-189.)

Again, be sure to check with your local elections board to determine the exact forms required in your state and the frequency with which you need to file them.

Planning for Victory

In order to plan for a victory the terms of the victory need to be definable. In election terms, you will need to know approximately how many votes it will take to win the race. While this might sound like something that is nearly impossible to do, there is a mathematical way to make a reasonable determination by studying historical data that is available through your local board of canvassers.

❖ First, determine how many voters are eligible to cast ballots in each polling place or precinct within the district. Then reduce that number by applying a factor of 10% to account for the number of faulty registrations.

NOTE: The voting lists in most jurisdictions include the names of people who have moved, are deceased, or changed

27

their name without asking that the registration under the original address or name be deleted. That means a person's name may appear on the voting rolls of two different precincts or twice on the same precinct under different names. All of these possibilities will artificially inflate the voting list.

❖ Next, ask the clerk of the board of canvassers for the percentage of voter turnout in the last 4 elections. If the clerk will not run the calculation for you the number can be determined by dividing the total number of people that voted in a particular year by the number of people eligible to vote based on the voting list of that same year.

➢ Getting the historical information for the past four elections will provide you with information from two presidential and two non-presidential elections. *NOTE: this will enable you to develop an expected voter turnout number regardless of whether you are running in a presidential year or not.* This is significant because a year in which the president is on the ballot generally has a greater voter turnout than a year in which the president is not running for election.

❖ Multiply that number by the adjusted number of eligible voters to reveal the anticipated voter turnout in your election. For example, if there are 2,000 eligible voters on the current voting list, and the historical data indicates an average four-year voter turnout of 54%, then you would apply the following calculation:

Registered voters (2,000) - adjustment factor (10%)
= 1,800 eligible voters

1,800 eligible voters x the historical four- year voter turnout
(assume 54% for this example)
= 972 voters

972 voters will be expected to vote in that precinct
in your election.

If you are running against one opponent, then you will need 487 votes (or 50.1%) to win that polling place in a two way contest.

❖ Repeat these steps for every polling place in your district and you will know approximately how many votes you will need to win the election. This information will also assist you in determining how many election-day give-a-way products you will need to provide to the volunteers working the exterior of each poll on election-day thereby allowing you to better plan your budget. *(More on that in chapter 7!)*

❖ Now that you know how many votes you will need to win, you can establish a goal to identify that number of supporters by election-day – those people that you have identified as a 1s and 2s on your walking sheets.

NOTE: walking sheets and the associated voter ranking system will be explained in detail in chapter 7, 10, 11 and 12

➢ If, for example, you know you will need 1,248 votes to win the election, you will want to try to identify a minimum of 1,248 people that were given a ranking of 1 or 2 on the walking sheets.

➢ On election-day, your volunteers will spend the day tracking those voters to be sure that they actually cast a vote. *(See Bingo System – chapters 11 and 12.)*

➢ If identified supporters have not voted by about 4:00 in the afternoon, your headquarters volunteers will start making phone calls to those people to remind them how important their vote is to the candidate and how he/she is really relying on that person's vote. *(This will also be explained in greater detail in chapters 7, 10, 11 and 12.)*

➢ Your volunteer should also check to see if the identified supporter will need a ride to the polls and if so, follow-up by arranging for a volunteer to pick him/her up and drive him/her to the polling place and back.

NOTE: this process is part of the "bingo system" and will be explained in great detail in chapters 10, 11 and 12.

Chapter 6
Developing Your Campaign Message

Defining Your Platform

❖ A platform is a compilation of issues that you will address during your campaign. Each individual issue of the platform is called a plank. Every candidate should develop a sound platform from which to launch his campaign.

❖ The planks should consist of both issues of concern to the people living in your district, issues that have been discussed in the recent past, but remain unresolved, as well as new, innovative ideas that will improve the quality of life for people living in your political jurisdiction and/or beyond. For example, if you are seeking a position on the town council your platform might include proposals that address the following issues:

> Trash collection and disposal
> Road resurfacing and pothole repair
> Holding the line on taxes or reducing the tax rate
> Adding, expanding or eliminating community policing options
> Instituting or expanding curbside recycling, etc.
> Ethics reform
> A means tested tax freeze for senior citizens

❖ Some of these issues may have been debated over the past couple of years but not resolved to the community's satisfaction while others may be brand new issues never considered by the incumbent or the council as a whole.

❖ Proposing a platform that addresses both lets the voters know that you understand the issues of the day, and that you are capable of thinking outside the box in ways that those currently holding office either can't or haven't. That will not only show that you are innovative, but it will imply, without you ever having to say it, that your opponent lacks innovation. It will set your candidacy apart from the candidacies of the opponents making you appear a logical choice to the voter.

❖ A candidate that has only a one-plank platform is known as a single issue candidate. While single-issue candidates have been known to win elections, they generally are not successful unless the single issue is one of overwhelming concern to a great majority of voters in the district and no other candidate shares the same view on it. Generally speaking, a candidate with a well-rounded and thought provoking multi-planked platform would have a much better chance of success.

If you are not able to define even a single-planked platform, then you might want to reconsider your candidacy. The inability to define a platform can be an indication that either all the issues are being adequately addressed by the current officials, or that you may be in a position to neither adequately recognize what needs to be done nor serve the residents from the position to which you aspire.

Crafting Your Message

Once you have determined the platform for your campaign, you will need to craft the campaign's message. Your message is the device you will use to inform your constituency as to why you are running for office and why you believe you are the best person to accomplish the objectives set forth in your platform.

❖ There are several things that should be considered in the message development process. The first of these is the identification of the demographic for which your message is intended. Demographic information includes identifiers such as ethnicity, age, gender, occupation, income and race. It also will identify if you have a voting population comprised predominantly of renters or homeowners, white collar or blue collar workers, Republicans, Democrats or Independents, etc. All of this information will help you determine which of the issues identified in your platform will have the greatest appeal to the voters that comprise your district and that is important information that will help you identify and prioritize the issues that you will spend your advertising dollars on.

➢ There are a couple of ways to collect the demographic information you need. The least expensive way is to review the census data for your district. The most efficient way, taking a professional poll, comes with a price tag. Either method, however, may provide you with enough information to craft an effective message.

❖ The issues that you address in your platform should be rooted in your personal philosophy and should not be developed simply to pander to a particular constituency. That is why I chose to address platform development before suggesting message development. However, the manner in which you inform voters of your position on various issues is all about political strategy.

Now that you have a campaign platform and message, it is time to develop the strategy for delivering that message.

Creating a Compelling Campaign Slogan

A campaign slogan doesn't cost anything, but it can be a very powerful tool that helps promote your message. In fact, the slogan should be tied directly to your message and should, in just a few short words, define your message.

❖ Create a slogan that will tug at the voter's emotional heart strings, drawing them to you as the person who can keep them safe or provide better schools or choice health care, etc. Choose values that most people tend to agree with rather than controversial words that are divisive.

❖ The best slogans are the ones that both evoke an emotional response, are reassuring and are memorable. In 1984 Ronald Reagan's slogan, *"It's Morning Again in America,"* gave folks a sense that a new day was dawning with better times ahead for all Americans. That is exactly what the voters longed for. Likewise, when Jimmy Carter opposed Gerald Ford following the "long national nightmare" that was Watergate and Ford's subsequent pardon of former President Richard Nixon, his slogan of, *"A Leader, For A Change"* instilled in voters a confidence in Carter's ability to lead and lead effectively.

❖ Once developed, use the slogan on everything associated with your campaign. Put it in your ads, on your fundraising tickets, letterhead, envelopes, business cards, website, bumper stickers, posters, emails, campaign buttons, press releases and anything else that your campaign offers the public.

Chapter 7
Effective Campaigning on a Budget

Campaigns generally come down to two main components - *name recognition* and *message delivery* – and, each can be very expensive. But just how much money you will need to finance your campaign depends upon a great number of variables. If you are already well known throughout the district in which you will be running you may not have to spend as much money on name recognition as you otherwise might and can focus that money on message delivery - informing voters that, if elected, you will be able to do a better job than the other candidates. On the other hand, if you are a relative unknown, you may need to spend a significant amount of money on name recognition - just telling voters who you are.

Regardless of how much money you will need to spend on various portions of the campaign, there are certain financial needs that every campaign will have to manage in successfully accomplishing the objectives of these two main components. While certainly not an exhaustive list, presented here are some traditional, tested and effective ways a candidate can promote his/her name and campaign message. Additional message delivery ideas and methods are limited only by your (and your committee's) imagination and creativity.

❖ **Brochures** – You should produce some written item that delivers the message of who you are and why you are running. A campaign brochure is like your political resume. It should be easy to understand yet comprehensive in nature. It should include several items not necessarily limited to the following:

➢ *Front cover design* that has your name, photo and position being sought identified by district or precinct number. IE, John P. Smith, Town Council District 4.

➢ *The interior* should include a *short biographical sketch* that addresses items such as your name, occupation, education received, church attended, family, etc.

➢ A *statement of purpose* – in other words, why are you running? Do you want to lower taxes, protect the environment, reform schools, improve ethics, etc. This short paragraph is an opportunity to point out the shortcomings of the incumbent office holder(s) without getting personal and discuss why you feel there's room for improvement. Let's face it, if things are fine just the way they are, then maybe you shouldn't be running unless of course you are running for an open seat and will, perhaps, continue the same policies as your predecessor.

NOTE: This area should contain a positive statement about you, not a negative statement about your opponent. For example, do not write, "George Jones has routinely raised your taxes while ignoring the deplorable conditions of our local streets." Write instead, "I intend to hold the line on taxes while initiating a comprehensive street repaving program that will ensure that every street in town is repaved within four years." This positive statement essentially implies that the current office-holder has done neither. Also note that this statement is general in nature. During the course of the campaign be prepared to address the specifics that will demonstrate how you can adopt such a program without the need for a tax increase.

➢ **Your Platform** – should consume the majority of your text. Here you will not only state each platform plank, but discuss in a sentence or two what you plan to do about it. For example, if you want to reduce taxes, it is not enough to say I will vote to reduce taxes. You should explain, in short bullet point sentences, the specific item(s) you intend to cut and why it won't negatively impact service delivery. For example, I will reduce spending by outsourcing waste collection and disposal services thereby reducing the cost by $35,000 per year.

Note: during the campaign you will need to show exactly how outsourcing this service will in fact save the amount of money you claim. This can be done through a combination of press releases and leaflet drops.

If you have 7 platform planks, list all 7 devoting a single bullet to each issue. No one bullet should exceed two or three sentences in length or you risk losing the reader's interest.

> ➤ A *final section might include community activities*. If you are a member of the local lions or Rotary club, church group, FOPA, little league organization, or if you have been volunteering as a basketball or soccer coach, etc. or for a state or national organization such as the American Cancer Society or the American Association of Planners, etc. list those activities along with your years of service and any offices you held or hold within the organizations.

> ➤ *The back cover* - can contain another photo, perhaps a family photo if you are so inclined. It should also repeat your name, the office being sought, the date of the election, where on the ballot your name will be found (if that information is known at publication time) and a plea for support. That last item is most important! Tip O'Neill, former Speaker of the United States House of Representatives, loved to tell the story about a neighbor who admitted not having voted for him. Surprised to hear that a woman that he had been so friendly with didn't support him, he asked why. She said simply, "Because you didn't ask me to." Always remember to ask for the vote both in writing and personally! You can never ask too much. Sometimes many of the items discussed for inclusion on the back cover are included in an "open letter" to the voters rather than as individually bulleted items. That is a very acceptable way to relay this information to the voters.

Brochures come in a variety of styles. They can be two sides of a single page, a bi-fold or tri-fold, a post card, etc. They can be printed in color or black and white, on glossy stock or plain copy paper. The style you choose will naturally depend on the budget you have available to you. Whichever style you choose, make sure all of the content is grammatically correct, easy-to-read, aesthetically pleasing, and in a font size that both old and young readers can easily see.

❖ **Leaflets** – also called "flyers," are a very cost-effective alternate means of message delivery. Flyers are not nearly as detailed as the brochure and generally address only one or two planks of your platform.

➢ In addition to addressing your platform planks, leaflets might also be "issue related." Issue related leaflets address specific issues of particular concern to a smaller constituency. For example, consider addressing issues of concern to the elderly or a leaflet intended for distribution at a senior citizen center or senior citizen housing complex. If flooding has been an issue in a certain neighborhood, consider a special leaflet addressing your approach to resolving it and distribute the flyer only on the impacted streets, etc.

➢ Unlike brochures, leaflets are often times a single or half sheet of 8.5 x 11 paper (or heavier stock if it is affordable), printed on a copy machine or computer printer, and distributed to every door in the impacted area. They are very cost effective because they are delivered by volunteers and can ensure a powerful impact if timed right.

➢ Leaflets are also effective for message delivery to the entire district. This delivery system is known as a *"leaflet drop"* and distribution is performed by a group of volunteers known on the campaign as *"leafleters."* Here's how a leaflet drop works:

✓ Select a date for the drop. A Saturday is usually a good day since most people don't have to work and the youngsters are not in school. In addition, you always have the option of using Sunday as a rain date should Saturday's weather not cooperate.

✓ An issue (platform plank) is selected by the media coordinator and other senior staff volunteers as the subject of the leaflet. The leaflet should address the specifics of the issue in relative detail but presented in easy to read, aesthetically pleasing fashion using creative bullet points. The leaflet also should boldly display the candidate's name, party affiliation and position sought.

✓ Make a sufficient number of copies and assemble them in individual packets (one packet for each leafleter) basing the quantity of each packet on the number of houses on the streets that each leafleter will be assigned. Be sure to include a set of instructions with each packet. Instructions should include a statement of conduct during the leaflet drop. These volunteers represent your campaign. They should be courteous and respectful to everyone they meet. They should avoid confrontation and not engage any resident in a partisan debate about you or your campaign. They should take notes of anyone they meet that comments on you or the campaign including a phone number if the voter wants the candidate to contact him/her. Bind the packet with an elastic band and label it with the names of the streets to be dropped, the name and contact information of the leafleter, and the time that the leafleter will pick up the packet from headquarters. Make a copy of the label that will be kept at headquarters.

✓ Try to enlist a sufficient number of leafleters to ensure that the entire district will be covered with no single leafleter having to walk more than 5 or 6 streets or work for more than one to two hours. Volunteers may get tired or discouraged if the route is too long causing them to either skip entire streets or certain houses on those streets.

✓ On the day of the drop, the volunteer leafleter will walk to every door on the assigned streets leaving a rolled or folded flyer in the door handle of the storm door or in another location that can be easily noticed by the homeowner.

NOTE: Volunteer leafleters must be instructed to avoid placing the leaflet in the US mailbox as it is a violation of federal law for anyone other than a postal worker to place items in someone's mailbox.

✓ If young volunteers are helping with the leaflet drop as they frequently do, they should either be assigned in pairs (for their own protection and to ensure that the leaflets are not discarded in the trash as opposed to being left in the voter's doors) and an older volunteer should drive them to their assigned location and pick them up when their drop has been completed.

✓   Instruct all volunteer leafleters to return to head-quarters when they have completed their assignment. At this time they can return any unused flyers as well as the instruction sheet showing which streets were completed. If any streets were not completed, other volunteers may be dispatched to those areas. Volunteers should also note any problems encountered or comments received during their leaflet drop.

Though labor intensive, the "leaflet drop" is a very effective information delivery method because it reaches every household within a matter of a couple of hours and cost nothing but the price of a making the copies. I always conducted at least two or three leaflet drops in each of my campaigns. They maintained volunteer involvement in the campaign, helped to make them stakeholders in the outcome, and saved significant amounts of money that might have otherwise been spent on mailings or newspaper advertisements.

On election eve we even leafleted cars parked on the street in front of houses in my district by placing the leaflet on the windshield of the vehicle secured by the driver's windshield wiper. We very quietly dropped the leaflets at or around midnight to ensure that the flyer wouldn't be removed by the opponent and would be the first thing the voter would see when he/she got in his/her vehicle on election morning. Our message on this ¼ page flyer was simple, *"Please remember to vote for Paul F. Caranci today. We are very grateful for your support."* These flyers were a great last minute reminder for the voter to vote and to vote for me.

❖   **Bumper stickers and political pins or buttons** – These items can be an effective way of both gaining name recognition and identifying supporters. They can also be

43

very expensive. Bumper stickers are purchased in minimum quantities which usually begin at 250 and can cost as much as $1.50 to $2.00 per sticker in quantities that small. If you do have the resources to purchase these items you should always opt for a quality vinyl sticker that is easily removed from the supporter's vehicle as opposed to old fashioned paper stickers which can be problematic in that regard. Many people don't like to litter their car with bumper stickers however and convincing enough people to effectively use 250 of them in a local race can be difficult and therefore wasteful. Some of my supporters would make a cardboard "tent," and place the sticker on one side. They would then place the "tent" on the rear console of the car with the sticker facing out the back window. I always asked supporters to place the sticker on the rear window however. In that location it is easier to read and remove without risking a scratch to a painted surface.

Like stickers, campaign pins or buttons can also be expensive. Many candidates have reverted to the use of paper "buttons" that are much more cost effective and meant to be worn during a specific event and then discarded. *(NOTE: when using "paper stickers" be sure to advise supporters not to stick them on certain elements of clothing. I have seen more than one person ruin a leather jacket or suede coat by affixing a lapel sticker to it.)*

If funding is not an issue however, bumper stickers and campaign pins/buttons can go a long way in helping to identify true supporters.

❖ **Lawn signs** - are a significantly important element to any campaign. They are highly visible and indicate the potential support of more than just one voter of the household. They can be intimidating to an opponent, particularly when you have several on the same street or in the same neighborhood. The signs can deliver almost any message that you wish to convey, but like the brochure, it should be designed so as to be easy to read and aesthetically pleasing to view.

➢ Signs come in several varieties of sizes, colors and materials, but while a bit more expensive, you should consider vinyl signs printed on two sides that slide over a metal rim and are easily inserted into the ground. Avoid cardboard signs that need to be stapled to wooden stakes.

➢ I believe that lawn signs are one of the most effective campaign tools available and would routinely invest a significant amount of my advertising budget in them. They are much more effective, in my opinion, than billboards because they are more personal.

➢ Signs used in my campaigns read *"Another family supporting Paul Caranci for Council,"* and were displayed on three lines with my name and position in larger letters than the 1st line. They were made in my town's colors (blue & gold) and I had as many as 300 on various lawns throughout my district.

➢ I even had about 4-5 corrugated plastic 4X8 signs made that read, *"Another neighborhood supporting Paul Caranci for Council."* These signs were strategically placed on lawns fronting highly travelled main roads throughout the district. Now the implication of those signs, that the entire neighborhood was supporting me, was very intimidating to my opponent!

✓ Placing the larger 4 X 8 signs generally require some tools and carpentry skills. If you have neither, solicit help from a volunteer who has them.

✓ The 4 X 8 signs are generally assembled with a 2 X 3 wood frame and legs inserted into pre-dug holes in the ground and secured and balanced using stakes made from furan strips.

❖ **Media advertising** – Advertising is a very expensive proposition but one that is generally necessary in the promotion of both name and message. There are many options available to a candidate. A few of the more prevalent choices are described here:

➢ **Television and Radio** - Most local campaigns do not advertise on television and radio because of the high cost. Although if affordable, those outlets are very effective means of both message delivery and name recognition. If you do choose to advertise this way, you will get the most "bang for your buck" if you keep the message short and make it straightforward.

✓ Before choosing a television or radio station with which to advertise you will want to be sure that the station/program you choose will reach the proper audience. For example, radio talk shows may provide either liberal or conservative programming. Music stations may target young or older listeners. Some may have a high rating (listening audience) while others may have very few listeners. These are all factors to consider when allocating your advertisement dollars. It is not worth advertising on a station that has less expensive rates if the message will not be heard by the intended audience. The same goes for television advertising. If you want to reach an older audience, you may not want to advertise on MTV. If, on the other hand your target audience is senior citizens, you may choose a daytime program or the nightly news as these are programs whose audience will tend to be older. Most radio and television media outlets will happily provide their demographic information upon request.

✓ Call the radio or television station and ask who you will need to meet with to discuss demographics. Make an appointment with that person to determine costs, deadlines, and other pertinent information. Radio and television ads require copy to be produced and delivered to the station in a format that can be aired on the station while print media will generally set the ad for you as part of the cost of ad placement. Consultants and public relations firms have the equipment and knowledge to provide you with air-ready copy for radio and television. If you are undertaking this task on your own, it is risky at best. You might also inquire with the station to see if they offer the service for you and at what cost. If you are going to spend the money to advertise on radio or television, be sure that you factor in the cost of production. Finally, the choice air time tends to be reserved early by large companies or major campaigns. Don't wait too long before reserving your selected time choice.

✓ Call local television and radio talk show hosts and inquire about being a guest on their shows. Such hosts may be particularly receptive to having you appear as a guest if your campaign proposed something unique or controversial. Don't be afraid to contact the show producers frequently asking for an opportunity to appear as a guest. Once accepted, you may be given a choice of being an "in-studio" guest or a "phone-in" guest. When possible, always choose to appear in the studio. The quality of your voice will be much better and you run less risk of being "cut off" by the host. Plus, if you impress the host you may be asked back!

✓ Make it a habit to call the radio talk shows and comment on the issue of the day, particularly if it is an issue of political importance to the people of your district. Always identify yourself using your first and last name so the audience becomes familiar with you. Be articulate, brief and try to periodically mention that you are a candidate for office.

➢ **Newspaper advertising**, particularly in local weekly newspaper publications, is much more affordable.

✓ The first thing you will need to do is to obtain or assemble a complete listing of all local print, radio and television media available in your district. If you are not able to acquire a complete list from other candidates or party officials, the internet or a member of a local social or sports organization may be a good source of that information. The list should include the media outlet, the address and phone number and the appropriate contact person and that person's title.

✓ Like the brochure and lawn sign, the newspaper ad should be uncluttered, aesthetically pleasing and easy to read. It should contain certain basic information such as your name, the position you are running for and your party affiliation. You might also consider including the date of the election especially if you are running in a special election being held at a time when people are not accustomed to voting. While some ads can provide good exposure with only the basic information, you might be better served by adding one or two planks from your platform as bullet points in the advertisement.

✓ Repetition is always a key element in advertising. Consequently, you should run an ad for 4-6 consecutive weeks. If you pay for all the ads at the same time, the salesperson may be able to reserve the same location in the paper for each advertisement. If you are given that option, take it. Likewise, it is best if the basic information (name, office sought, etc.) in the ad is the same each week changing only the planks from ad to advertisement. After a few weeks, the reader will begin to recognize your ad by the location and style alone. If you are able to place multiple ads during the campaign, the newspaper may offer discounts if you order and pay for the ads in advance. The ad copy can be provided in accordance with the publications deadlines. Make a point of asking when those deadlines are and be aware that during weeks in which there is a holiday, the deadline may be moved up.

✓ It is always most desirable to place your ad on the right side page of the open paper and at the top right corner of that page because that is the first place the reader's eye goes when a page is turned. If it is available and affordable to you, the back cover is also a great location for your ad, but that page is sometimes reserved for a full page ad and is generally significantly more expensive than an interior advertisement. Few papers allow advertisements on the front page but if your paper allows for it, that is also a highly desirable location for an advertisement. The centerfold is another great ad location, but it may also come at a premium price.

✓ Some jurisdictions may have small, inexpensive ad publications such as The Penny Pincher or similar type "ad" publications that are given away free to consumers and are available at a variety of retail outlets. These publications generally contain coupons and information for consumers and are widely viewed by people in a small locale. Before advertising in such a publication, however, ask how many distribution outlets are located in your district and how many copies are distributed at each of those outlets each week. If the readership doesn't warrant it, don't spend your money there.

> ➤ **Cable Television** - may also have some inexpensive advertising opportunities, particularly local "interconnect" stations. If viewership warrants, consider advertising there as well. Simply call your local cable company and inquire about advertising opportunities.

   ✓ Some cable companies have studios available for local use and, after taking a short "class" on the instruction of their use, they may allow these facilities to be used to produce a television spot that may later be used as an advertisement for traditional television.

   ✓ Many cable companies allow local access channels that are dedicated to community services. If possible, consider hosting your own cable television show that provides information of interest to the local community in which you want to run. It would be advisable to get permission to do this prior to announcing your candidacy as you don't want it to appear that you are doing this simply as a means of promoting your candidacy as programming for that specific purpose may be prohibited.

   NOTE: Check your local cable stations rules and regulations as well as state or local laws governing a candidate's use of cable television this way. You want to be sure not to run afoul of any campaign laws.

Here's one final word of advice regarding campaign advertising. Take advantage of every free opportunity to promote your candidacy. Ask local organizations such as the Rotary Club, the

Lions Club, the FOPA, local church groups and sports organizations if you can speak to their members at one of their meetings. No group is too insignificant and no audience too small to help you spread your message. If you can be a guest speaker at one of their weekly or monthly meetings do it, as even an audience as small as 4 or 5 people will hear your message and tell others how impressive you are or how attractive your platform is.

❖ **Door-to-door canvassing** – is an essential element of a local campaign and, fortunately, it is free, save perhaps the cost of replacing a pair of shoes that may wear out along the way. Canvassing the district involves walking to each residential door on every street, meeting voters, introducing them to your candidacy and asking them to support you if after reading your literature they believe you can improve the quality of life for the town. Depending on the size of your district, you may even consider walking to every door twice.

  ➢ *Walking Sheets* - To prepare for your canvassing efforts you will need to develop a walking sheet. This sheet will provide the names and addresses of each voter in your district as well as a ranking system that will become a vital part of the bingo system that you will use on election-day. *(More on the bingo system in chapters 11 and 12)* Preparing walking sheets will be a time consuming task that should begin as early as practicable. There is a very specific design that you should use to develop the walking sheet. That design, and information on how the walking sheet works is described here:

  ✓ Make a separate sheet(s) for each street in your district and arrange the houses numerically. For example, the walking sheet(s) for "Smith Street" should contain the house number for each house on the street starting with 1 Smith St. and ending with 126 Smith St. if that is the number of the last house on the street.

✓ List the name of each voter within every household on the sheet in alphabetical order.

✓ Write the numbers 1-5 to the right of each voter's name. These numbers represent the rankings you will use to evaluate every voter you meet.

- If the voter tells you that he/she will support you with a lawn sign, bumper sticker and/or a campaign contribution, or if he/she has signed your nomination papers, then circle #1.

- If the voter indicates that you will get their vote, but doesn't offer a sign location, sticker or contribution, then circle #2.

- If you are unable to gauge who the voter will support after your brief conversation with him/her, then circle #3.

- If the voter indicates that he likes the opponent or may not like you, then circle #4.

- If the voter is displaying your opponent's lawn sign or bumper sticker, then circle #5.

NOTE: try to determine who in the house is supporting the opponent as it is possible that one member of the household is supporting the opponent while another member might prefer you. Don't write off the entire family simply because of a lawn sign.

SAMPLE WALKING SHEET

Walking Sheet Smith Street			
Voter's Name	Date Visited	Ranking	Comments
1 Jones, John	July 14th	1 2 3 4 5 NH	Interested in street repaving
Mary	July 14th	1 2 3 4 5 NH	Complained about schools
Joseph	July 14th	1 2 3 4 5 NH	Senior in high school
2 Zurretti, Steven	July 14th	1 2 3 4 5 NH	Retired last year
Pauline	July 14th	1 2 3 4 5 NH	Hasn't voted in last 4 elections
3 Manchester, Robert	July 14th	1 2 3 4 5 NH	single dad, asked for a lawn sign
Joey	July 14th	1 2 3 4 5 NH	in school w/my opponent's daughter and is supporting him.
4 Smith, James	July 14th	1 2 3 4 5 NH	
Beatrice	July 14th	1 2 3 4 5 NH	

✓ Over the course of the campaign you will hope-fully have a significant number of 1s and 2s. These are your supporters and you will want to ensure that they vote on election-day. *NOTE: There will be more details on getting out the vote in chapters 10 and 11.*

✓ The 3s are undecided voters and you have as much of a chance of earning their vote as your opponent does. These are the voters that you may want to contact several times throughout the campaign. You can walk to their door a 2nd or 3rd time, have a special mailing to them, call them on the telephone, or any other strategy you can employ to win their approval and support. On election day, after you are sure that all your 1s and 2s have voted, concentrate on getting the 3s out to vote. To accomplish this, the volunteers will need to call all the 1s, 2s, and 3s that have not voted by a certain time on election-day. Therefore, the volunteers will need to collect phone numbers for any 1, 2 or 3 that you have identified.

NOTE: This process, known as the "bingo system" will be discussed in greater detail in chapters 10 and 11.

Finally, don't assume that simply because one family member is supporting you, all the other members of the household will support you too. Families often fail to agree on who they will support and end up splitting their vote. Therefore, unless you have been told that a person is supporting you don't label them with a one or two. If you do, your volunteers may just be calling your opponent's supporters on election day reminding them to get out and vote!

❖ **Coffee hours** – a coffee hour is an event that usually takes place in someone's home, including senior citizen housing, in which the candidate meets prospective voters. In a typical coffee hour the "host" invites his/her friends and neighbors to come to his/her home on a certain day at a certain time to meet you. It is like a very informal house party and guests may receive a verbal or written invitation that is mailed in advance of the event by the host. If the host doesn't have time to prepare the invitations, a campaign volunteer can do that using a list provided by the host. If a volunteer does prepare the invitations, the host should still sign his/her own name. These events constitute a great opportunity to meet new voters in a comfortable setting, talk to them one-on-one, and address their specific concerns or answer their specific questions. Because it is so informal, it affords you an opportunity to befriend the attendees and help gain their confidence. Take advantage of as many of these events as you can schedule.

➤ You should always attend a coffee hour with a volunteer who can assist you with distributing lawn signs and bumper stickers and enlisting volunteers to support you in the campaign either financially or as a volunteer, even if only on election day.

➤ At the event you will have a chance to meet the guests and speak with them either individually, as a group or both. Always distribute your brochures to the attendees early in the hope that they might have time to read through it and ask you any questions while you are there. This is a great opportunity for you to shine and impress the voters with your confidence, your knowledge, your speaking style and your platform. Keep the speech short but cover the important points and be sure to respond to questions. Publicly thank the host for having you in his/her home and the guests for taking the time to attend. Ask for their vote and their help during the campaign and on election day.

➢ Coffee hours held at senior citizen homes are similar but may become more elaborate affairs. They are often times organized by a resident of the housing complex and generally with the permission of the complex manager. Frequently, it is up to your campaign staff to prepare and bring food and/or pastry, coffee and beverages.

✓ Some of the events we held during my council campaigns were quite elaborate affairs with each candidate trying to "outdo" the other in an effort to impress the residents. What began as a coffee and pastry event soon developed into a 4 or 5 course meal. The extreme is not necessary, but if it's affordable, it certainly doesn't hurt your chances of gaining the support of those in attendance.

➢ Sometimes, several candidates with similar political views may collaborate on sponsoring these events. They certainly become more manageable and affordable that way.

➢ The preparation, the event itself and the clean-up can be labor intensive. Some complexes have kitchens and allow you to cook on site. Other facilities require that all the cooking be done at another location and carried into the complex. Be certain that you have enough volunteers to execute the event or it may be a complete flop that will end up hurting rather than helping your candidacy. Try to maintain one specific group of volunteers for this purpose as after holding one or two of these events it becomes a routine that is easily handled.

➢ It is very important that you be on time especially if you are providing lunch or dinner for the residents. It is equally important that you be entertaining, not boring, in your presentation. You want to stand out in the resident's minds so that they will remember you above all the other candidates that have visited them. Senior citizens do talk to each other and you want the talk about you and your event to be positive.

- Let me tell a quick anecdotal story about senior citizen coffee hours. One candidate running for state representative that used to campaign with me at senior citizen coffee hours (I had 7 high rises in my council district) must have read a memory book. He used his name recall to his great advantage. Prior to the start of the event he would walk to each senior citizen and introduce himself saying, *"If I remember your name at the end of the event, will you remember my name on election day?"* Of course everyone agreed. About an hour later, as he was winding up his remarks he would say, *"OK, you all made me a promise at the beginning of the night,"* and he would repeat the agreement. Then he would proceed to name every person in the room in the order in which they sat at their tables. He never missed a name and it so impressed the seniors (and every other candidate in the room) that it became the topic of conversation at every other event for the balance of the campaign season! Because of that, I remember those events vividly even after all these years.

❖ **Debates** – may or may not be necessary depending on the position you are running for. Many times debates are organized by outside, non-partisan groups such as the League of Women Voters, Common Cause or some other good government group. Generally debates are not planned for school committee seats while debates for council positions are sometimes scheduled. Those running for mayor will almost always be involved in a debate, maybe even two.

➤ If debates are not scheduled by an independent group for a position that you are seeking, you can always issue your own debate challenge.

➤ If you are running against an incumbent candidate, it is a pretty good idea to issue a debate challenge.

✓ The incumbent probably won't accept the challenge as he/she will have no interest in giving you any additional exposure. If however you are able to arrange for a debate, be sure to pay attention to the details of the event and try to insist on a format that you are most comfortable with.

• There are many details that need to be addressed when setting up the debate. For example, will you stand at a podium or will you be seated?

• If seated, will you sit on stools or in easy chairs?

- Will you be seated behind a table or simply on a stage?

- Will you be provided time for an opening and closing statement, or will you be asked questions for the entire length of the debate?

- Will you debate for an hour, less or more?

- Will you be allowed to have and take notes?

- Will you be allowed to rebut your opponent's remarks and will there be time for a response to the rebuttal?

- Who will moderate the event?

- Will there be a live audience?

- Will the event be televised?

- Will you be asked questions posed by the audience or will all questions come from the moderator?

- Etc, etc, etc.

These are all issues that will need to be discussed and agreed to by the candidates before the candidates agree to participate in a debate. In preparation, determine the format that **you** would prefer and then do your best to insist that it happen that way.

> At the debate, always be respectful to the moderator and your opponent(s). Be humble but confident and

don't let the opponent or the crowd intimidate you. Never lose your cool! Try to smile as you talk, and practice, practice, practice, particularly the opening and closing statements. You don't want to have to read those statements because the words will tend to lose sincerity. You want the words to flow naturally (or at least appear that way) and come from the heart.

❖ **Building An Effective Website** – When I first ran for public office personal computers were in their infancy and Al Gore had not yet invented the internet! Today a website is an essential tool in the promotion of business and politics and neither can expect to be wildly successful without one.

➢ Websites can cost upwards of $1,000 for professional development or can be done for free using some Internet based site models. A tech-savvy volunteer can probably build a pretty effective campaign website for just the very small annual hosting fee typically about $100.00 using Weebly or GoDaddy, etc.

➢ The site should have an eye catching banner that includes your name, the position sought and campaign slogan.

➢ "Buttons" that open new pages should include press releases, position papers, events, volunteers, donations, photographs, videos, campaign schedule, and anything else considered vital to your personal campaign.

➤ Convert any video footage of your campaign to "YouTube" and create your own YouTube page. Effectively use Facebook and other social media outlets to promote your candidacy and website.

Be sure that the website is updated frequently so it contains the most current news of the campaign. There is nothing more disheartening to someone following your campaign via your website than to find nothing but stale news each time the site is accessed. There should be a volunteer dedicated to the job of keeping the information on your website current, fresh and interesting.

❖ **Fundraising** – One of the hardest campaign tasks I ever engaged in was asking people for money. Yet, raising adequate funds to run an effective campaign is one of the most important functions of a candidate, especially since candidates for local office generally can't afford to hire professional fund raisers. In order to maximize the campaign's fundraising potential you need to develop a fundraising plan. A formal plan will help you focus on the task, establish deadlines and meet them, and provide a standard by which you will be able to measure your progress.

There are several ways to raise money. Some of the more popular examples will be discussed here.

➤ *Direct mail solicitation* – involves sending letters asking the recipient to donate money to your campaign. Be specific in the letter about why you are asking, what you intend to use the money for, and a suggested amount that you are requesting.

✓ Always give the recipient options to donate varying amounts. For example, ask for a donation of $100, $50 or $25.

✓ If possible, enlist a service that will enable you to accept credit card donations.

✓ More than once I sent a couple of "free admission tickets" to an upcoming event, tickets that were donated to my campaign, with a letter requesting a donation and explaining that I would prefer that the recipient spend some quality time with his family by attending the event with them rather than spending a few hours with me at a boring reception. I generally got a good response to those solicitations and all it cost me was the price of sending a letter.

➢ *Telephone solicitation* – involves calling friends, relatives, supporters, business owners, etc. and asking them to contribute to your campaign.

✓ Just as is the case with direct mail, let the person you are soliciting by telephone know why you are asking for a donation and what the funds will be used for. Ask for a higher amount and if the prospect sounds hesitant, suggest a smaller amount. Keep reducing the amount being requested until you get a yes. Be sure to thank the prospect enthusiastically regardless of the size of the donation.

- A sample telephone solicitation might sound like this: *"Hi Joe, this is Paul Caranci. I hope you have been well and that everything is ok with your family. As you know I am running for town council. I decided to run because for so many years, our taxes just seem to be increasing but we never seem to notice any improvement in our services. Crime is up, streets are in disrepair and even our trash isn't being collected on a regular basis. I started to complain about it but then figured that I shouldn't complain if I'm not willing to help straighten out the mess. But I found that getting my message out to the voters takes a lot of money, a lot more than I am able to kick in from my own pocket. To help with message delivery I am calling some friends and family members to ask for a donation. I know that times are tough, but I think it's really important to start to turn the town around so that the average taxpaying resident can start to get a break too. Do you think you could help me out with a $100 donation to my campaign?"* If he hesitates for a few seconds or indicates that he cannot donate that much, then say, *"Would it be possible to donate $50?"* If he responds yes to any amount, say, *"Thank you Joe, I am very grateful. The next deadline for finance reporting is next Tuesday. Do you think you could send a check before then?"*

✓ Provide the address where the check can be sent and always suggest a date by which you will need the money, generally a date that coincides with the end of a reporting period at your local elections board, but not a date that is too far off into the future as the donor may forget if he/she is given too much time to write the check.

✓ It is important to collect all donations in time to meet the upcoming reporting deadline because the more money your report indicates that you have, the more momentum it appears your campaign is gaining and the more likely you may attract some big endorsements or contributions. After all, everyone likes a winner!

➢ *Fundraising Reception* – these events are generally held at a restaurant or hall and are ticketed events. Food and soft drinks are provided and alcoholic beverages may be served or made available at a cash bar.

✓ Ticket prices for fundraising receptions vary widely depending upon several factors including the economy, the office you are seeking, the financial ability of those invited, the quality of the establishment, the type of food offered, whether there will be an open or cash bar, etc.

• Consider a range of ticket prices. For example, Platinum Sponsor - $100, Sponsor - $75, Friend - $50. Another alternative is to write "*Suggested Donation - $100*" on the ticket and leave it up to the purchaser to decide the amount of the donation.

✓ Tickets should be mailed at least two weeks in advance of the event. You might consider placing an ad in a local paper with the ticket information as the ad copy if funds allow or if you don't have a large fundraising list of donors.

✓ You will have the option of speaking or not speaking at the event. I personally never liked a formal speech at my fundraising events preferring instead to speak to the guests one-on-one. That way, it wasn't boring to those not particularly interested in politics, but provided everyone an opportunity to ask questions important to them or to ask for a favor if that was the reason they attended.

✓ You should enlist the services of a volunteer or two to sit at a table by the door to accept paid tickets or donations.

• Some candidates use a number board to keep track of paid tickets. I always preferred to simply have the volunteer accept whatever is handed to them as the guest enters the hall. If someone is going to try to come in without paying, do you really want to make an embarrassing scene at your own event? Chances are that they will be allowed in whether their ticket number shows on the number board as paid or not, so why waste the time and risk creating the log jam at the door?

✓ As the candidate, I never strayed too far from the door. That way I could greet each person as they entered and thank them for their support.

✓ I was sure to always carry a notepad in my suit jacket pocket so I could take a note of any request that a guest had of me during the event, and believe me, I got many!

- Always be sure to follow up by providing whatever information is requested of you. Following up means that you will need to take a phone number and address of the person. Be sure to add that information to your fundraising database.

✓ Always send a thank you note to everyone that attended or donated to your events.

➤ *Chain Letters* – This is a classic form of fundraiser in which your campaign volunteers will each mail letters to their friends and relatives asking them to send you a small donation – maybe $10.00, and to send out 10 letters to their family members and friends requesting that they too send you $10.00 and keep the chain going. Each generation recipient will continue to send out letters to their friends and relatives and so on. The requested donation is relatively small and "the ask" is from a family member or friend so there is a reasonably good chance that you will actually receive a fair return from the first couple of generations of letters.

➤ *Fun Family Events* – One of my first fundraisers was a Halloween costume party. I held it in a Knights of Columbus hall that I rented for $35.00 and I brought in some food that my family whipped up and inexpensive snack foods and soft drinks that I purchased.

There was a cash bar operated by the Knights. We sold over 100 tickets for $5.00 each (1982 dollars) and collected over $500 in profits. We still have a good laugh when looking back at the old photographs. Other ideas are a roller-skating party, paint-ball party, miniature golf party, whiffle-ball home run derby, and any fun activity that most people can participate in regardless of age. These are fun family events and bringing the family means more money in your campaign account.

> *Website and Internet Money Bombs* – These events are gaining in popularity. They don't involve significant time and require very little planning. A fundraising goal is established for a specific purpose. For example, if you want to purchase bumper stickers which cost $500, then promote a money bomb on your campaign website and social media sites several weeks before the day indicating that you need to raise $500 to purchase campaign bumper stickers today on May 1st. On the appointed day, send out several email and social media blasts reminding people of your fundraising goal and the purpose for which you need the funds. When the event ends, be sure to announce the result and thank everyone for their support and efforts. In addition to paying for the stickers, you have just made effective use of social media to garner name recognition.

> *Build an On-line Network for Fundraising* – This is exactly what it sounds like and is a process that was perfected by Barack Obama in his 2008 presidential campaign. The result depends upon your "reach" - that is, the number of people you are connected with

on the various social media and internet sites. President Obama had a network that enabled him to send over a billion emails. Understandably, you don't have that kind of reach. Neither are you trying to raise the $650 million that Obama raised in his 2008 campaign. Even with your much smaller reach, you should be able to raise a decent percentage of the needed funds in this manner. Organize your contact database and use it to effectively raise money for your campaign. Then use the system you create to expand your database.

✓ To raise funds on-line you will need an on-line processing company that can accept your on-line donations. Be sure to shop around for the right processing company for your fundraising needs. Don't select a company that will take 15 or 20% of your contributions or charge exorbitant set-up fees. Be careful with monthly maintenance fees, per-transaction fees, etc. Discuss with the vendor the amount of money you plan to raise in this fashion and ask for the vendor's best options to help you achieve your goals. Don't commit during that phone call. Tell him you will need to discuss the details with your committee in order to buy time and continue to check with other companies. The wrong selection could doom the entire fundraising effort.

✓ Set up the system that allows supporters to donate. Don't make it complicated. The less information or clicks the better. The process has to be easily navigable for those that are tech-savvy as well as those that are not. The best approach is to place a "contribute" box or button right on the main page of a website where it is very easy to find.

NOTE: This same system can be used on your website to allow people to make other donations and pay for event tickets.

❖ <u>**Election-day at the polling places**</u> – Although it may seem like light years away, election-day will be here before you know it. You will need to save a little money to fund those activities that will take place that day. There are two that come to mind.

➢ You will want to have a presence at each polling place and you will want that presence from the moment the polls open until the very minute that they close.

✓ It is customary in most jurisdictions to have a volunteer standing outside the polling place either holding a sign bearing the candidates name and office being sought, or handing some type of give-a-way to each voter. The latter activity seems to be more prevalent in the northeastern part of the country, but it is practiced in multiple political jurisdictions throughout the United States.

• Depending on the give-a-way selected, the cost can be high. Many people hand out a simple flyer or palm-card with the candidates name and office and a last minute plea of support or a sample ballot reduced to the size of a palm card.

- Voters are sometimes annoyed passing through the gauntlet of candidates and the papers they are handed are generally discarded without even being read. Your volunteers need to be sensitive to the voter's reaction.

- A more productive idea is to distribute something of value to each voter. I have seen pens, pencils, rulers, bookmarks, flash drives, key chains, combs, and a variety of other novelty items. For the most part they are usable items and everyone loves a gadget!

  o These items are imprinted with the name and office of the candidate and a plea for support. If the item is not imprinted, then it is in a bag, or attached to a card that is imprinted. For example a pen may read, "Vote for John Smith – Councilman."

  o These items can cost anywhere from fifty cents each to $1.25 or more depending on which item you select and the quantity ordered.

  o If your budget allows, order enough pieces for every polling place based on an expected turnout of 50% or 60% of the eligible vote at each polling place. In years in which the president or a hotly contested congressional, state or local race is taking place, expect the turnout to be a little higher than normal. Your local board of

71

canvassers generally keeps historical information relative to election-day turnout. If they do not have the information, your local newspaper might.

NOTE: Refer to chapter 6 for details on how to project voter turnout in your election.

- Don't be afraid to get creative with your give-a-way item. One year I purchased individually wrapped fortune cookies from a company in California and stapled the wrapper to a post card with my picture, name and position sought emblazoned on it. Most every voter wanted one. Most read and discarded the post card and consumed the fortune cookie on their way into the poll. Almost everyone read the fortune, which was *"Please support Paul Caranci for council - your lucky numbers are ..."* The fortune cookies were a great hit.

Now I would not suggest that someone would vote for you simply because you gave them a pen or a cookie, but it certainly got me noticed by each voter coming into the polling place and it clearly made my message one of the last they saw prior to casting their vote. Regardless of which method you decide is best and most affordable for your campaign, be cognizant of the need to have some type of presence at the polls on election-day.

Chapter 8
Campaign Committee Development

Volunteers

It is virtually impossible to run an effective campaign without volunteers, but volunteers are sometimes hard to find. Initially, you may have to rely on family and very close friends, but once your campaign swings into high gear you should notice others either offering to assist or responding favorably to your request for help. There are plenty of jobs that you will need campaign volunteers to perform so that your time will be freed up for campaigning. Volunteer staff appointments, in no particular order, may include:

> ➤ **Campaign Coordinator** – This is the volunteer that coordinates the details of all campaign activities and

its events, tends to the daily activities of the campaign such as ensuring that: headquarters is adequately staffed, stolen or lost signs are promptly replaced, etc. This person would also suggest media events, assists with platform development, and participates in just about every other element of the campaign. Nothing in the campaign should be done without the campaign coordinator's approval and he/she must be in constant contact with the candidate.

> *Scheduler* – The scheduler works very closely with the candidate and is intimately familiar with the candidate's daily schedule enabling him/her to schedule new events that will not conflict with other elements of the schedule.

> *Campaign Manager* – The campaign manager is more of a figurehead and is selected for political reasons. The selected person may be a very prominent and popular former elected official. The manager may also be the opposite of the candidate in a variety of ways. For example, if you are a male candidate, you may want to consider a prominent female as your campaign manager. Likewise you may want someone of a different ethnicity, political persuasion or philosophy, etc. This diversity generally provides a balance to the campaign that might otherwise be lacking. If you can find someone that fits the bill and is willing to be an active participant in your campaign, that is certainly a bonus!

❖ *Treasurer* – As mentioned earlier, the treasurer will keep track of all contributions and expenditures, file timely campaign finance reports, and otherwise ensure compliance with all fundraising laws.

❖ *Media Specialist* – this is another position of critically high importance. This volunteer will draft press releases, arrange for media interviews, participate in candidate debate prep, and respond to all media inquiries. The media specialist will often times speak to the media for, and in place of, the candidate when the candidate is not available or chooses not to give comment directly.

❖ *Website Designer* – This volunteer will design an attractive and informative campaign website, arrange for its hosting and provide the updates as needed. The website designer should be media savvy and able to convert short videos of the candidate into You-Tube videos that are uploaded to the website following each event. This position works closely with the media specialist in this regard. The two positions may even be combined into one.

❖ *Legal Advisor* – Should be an attorney who will be able to advise you on any issue involving the law, particularly election law. If you are lucky, you will never need to call on him/her throughout the entire campaign. But if you find there's an issue, you will certainly be happy that you have identified someone you can call at a moment's notice, particularly on election-day where a 2 or 3 hour delay in addressing an issue could cost you the election.

❖ *Debate Preparation Team* – This group should include the campaign manager, campaign coordinator, media specialist, legal counsel and other trusted advisors. It should be a manageable group of no more than 4 or 5 people who will help you develop your debate message and quiz you as the moderator or others might during the debate.

❖ *Volunteer Coordinator* – The person assigned to keep the complete list of volunteers, their contact information, availability and assignments. The volunteer coordinator will also assure that sufficient volunteers are available for each specific task required for a successful campaign, particularly the election-day activities and events.

❖ *Senior Citizen Coordinator* – This person will coordinate any events having to do with senior citizens, such as coffee hours in senior citizen complexes, shut-in and absentee ballot applications and submissions, identifying those who may need a ride to the polls on election-day and arranging adequate transportation, etc.

❖ *Advance* – is another very important job throughout the campaign. The Advance coordinator will arrive at each scheduled event about an hour before the candidate to ensure that everything is in order. This person is generally responsible for working with the volunteer coordinator to ensure that there is an adequate crowd at every event at which the candidate will make an appearance. He/she will scan the crowd and take note of any dignitaries that the candidate will need to recognize, jotting down the names and passing them along to the candidate when he/she arrives. If you are not fortunate enough to have two advance people, then, on days in which there are multiple events, the advance person will leave the first event once the candidate has arrived, been briefed and is assured that everything is under control, so he/she can arrive at the next event an hour or so prior to the arrival of the candidate.

❖ *Sign Crew* – This is generally a blue-collar group of carpenters or handy-men that will erect large signs and install lawn signs. The majority of their work will take place over a very short period of time relatively early on in the campaign although they will be needed throughout the campaign to replace lost or stolen signs and/or repair damaged signs.

❖ *Social Media Host* – This is the person that will be responsible for daily blogging and posting to all social media sites including, but not limited to, Twitter, Facebook and Linked-in. The posts should be clean, crisp, exciting and easy to read snippets of the candidate's activities and should contain links to videos, the website, etc.

❖ *Bingo Coordinator* – This is a critically important position that coordinates the entire Bingo System that will be used on election-day both at headquarters and in the various polling places. This includes oversight of the Bingo preparation prior to election-day as well as the assignment and coordination of all workers needed to execute the Bingo System.

❖ *Inside Poll Workers – Bingo Checkers* – These volunteers will work in shifts taking names of those who have voted and recording the corresponding bingo number on bingo sheets that will be picked up each hour by the bingo poll runner.

❖ *Bingo Poll Runner* – This is the person(s) that will circulate to each polling place at least once an hour on election-day, collect the bingo sheets from the bingo checkers and return them to headquarters for recording by the headquarters bingo volunteers. This person can also be used to deliver meals and drinks to poll workers throughout the day since he/she will be making routine hourly stops at each polling place.

❖ *Outside Poll Workers – Visibility* – These are the volunteers that will staff the polls either holding signs or distributing your chosen give-a-way item to voters. They should be well dressed, and polite and they should ask each voter to consider your candidacy.

❖ *Coffee Hour Hosts* – These are the volunteers that will host, and procure other hosts, for coffee hours in the homes of supporters.

❖ *Fundraising Coordinator* – This person will arrange for a fundraiser host committee and the volunteers to stuff, seal and stamp the ticket envelopes. The fundraising coordinator will also keep track of those attending the event(s), prepare the ticket number board if you choose to have one at the door of the reception, ensure that the hall is decorated and the food and drink is fresh, hot/cold, set up before the start of the event, etc. This volunteer may also solicit a "reception committee." A reception committee is a group of people that will allow their names to be used on the fundraising ticket or on the fundraising letterhead.

NOTE: names of reception committee members are generally names only. They do not actually have to do any work on the reception planning, but usually will purchase a ticket and attend the event. Names should be listed down the side of the letterhead or ticket in such a way as to make the support seem overwhelming. They should include both prominent members of the community as well as the average supporter. This is a psychological

78

strategy that, if done right, can have a powerful impact, particularly on the opponent.

❖ **General Headquarters Volunteer Staff** – Any day-to-day requirements will be performed by this volunteer staff. Their duties might include looking up phone numbers for supporters identified on your walking sheets (numbers 1, 2 and 3), making copies, calling volunteers needed for specific events, etc.

NOTE: If nothing else, these are the people who will show up from day to day so that the headquarters never appears to be empty and without volunteer support. This can be another powerful psychological ploy that intimidates and/or demoralizes the opponent and his/her supporters.

❖ **Leafelters** – *These volunteers may work only one, two or three days of the campaign (depending on how many leaflet-drops you plan to have) but significant numbers of them are vital if you hope to complete the leaflet drop(s) within a reasonable timeframe. Generally they are youngsters (some of my leafleters were as young as 7-8 but were accompanied by an adult who drove them to their assigned area and followed behind them in a car.)*

Volunteers can be hard to come by, particularly in a local race. Therefore, it may be necessary for your volunteers to assume more than one role in the campaign. Often times, volunteers must fill multiple roles to ensure that every task is meticulously carried out. While some jobs require a unique talent or expertise, there are other positions that most anyone can handle. Certainly anyone working as a volunteer can leaflet or help out at a coffee hour.

Any single activity or event may be the only exposure that a voter has to your candidacy and it is possible you will be judged on that single event or by that one contact. It is critically important therefore that every activity and event be executed flawlessly and impressively. You may also find that you do not have enough volunteers to perform all of the functions even after doubling up some of the jobs. In that case you may have to eliminate an activity or event. The purpose of listing all the various campaign jobs is to give you an idea of what the ideal campaign will look like. It is rare that the ideal campaign becomes a reality. Don't sweat it. Do those things that you can and do them well. Don't worry about those things you are not able to do.

Volunteer Screening and Training

Every person who holds themselves out as a volunteer for your campaign and/or a supporter of your candidacy is assumed to be working on your behalf. Therefore, the manner in which he/she conducts him/herself will reflect on you. It is up to you and your campaign manager and coordinator to train the volunteers in their duties. At the very least, training should include the following:

❖ The volunteers should be dressed appropriately at all times that they are working for you.

❖ They should be courteous and pleasant at all times and never speak ill of your opponents or anyone else in public.

❖ They should be emphatically told that they are never to represent your positions without either having a written position paper from the campaign or without specific permission from the candidate or campaign manager. This applies to everything from talking to a voter to speaking to the press.

80

❖ Everything that a volunteer does, even something the volunteer does on his/her own time, can have severe repercussions on the campaign.

❖ For the reason stated in the previous bullet, volunteers need to be screened unless they are intimately known by the candidate.

> ➢ At the very least, conduct a google search of each volunteer.

> ➢ Ask for and check a reference or two.

> ➢ It is advisable to have every volunteer complete an application that is kept on file in the event that something from that volunteer's past surfaces during the campaign you will be able to demonstrate that the volunteer withheld the information from you.

> ➢ Be sure to alert the volunteer, in writing on the application form that he/she will be subject to a background review. Have the volunteer sign the volunteer application form acknowledging and authorizing that fact.

Ultimately the candidate will be held accountable for the behavior of the volunteers even if their negative deed was authorized by neither the candidate nor the campaign. By conducting a background check on each volunteer the candidate will at least be able to demonstrate that he did a careful and thoughtful review of the volunteer prior to allowing that person to represent him in the campaign. This provision should apply to every volunteer from the campaign coordinator to the election-day runner.

Volunteer Credentials

Certain volunteer activities generally require some type of credentialing. Determine which volunteers will need to have credentials and how those credentials are obtained in your local jurisdiction. Failing to provide the proper credentials may disqualify the volunteer from performing the campaign functions that he/she was assigned. That could have a detrimental impact on your campaign effectiveness and success.

❖ Volunteers who will work inside the poll on election-day are generally required to have credentials issued by the local board of canvassers. There is usually a period of time in which a candidate may submit a list of names to the local board of canvassers and credentials are issued sometime between that deadline and election-day.

➤ Call to check on the specific requirements of your local jurisdiction. Be sure a very trustworthy volunteer delivers the list of names that is prepared by the volunteer coordinator to the clerk of the board.

➤ It is never a bad idea to ask for a receipt. At the very least, keep a copy of every page you submit in the event the package was lost in transmission.

➤ When you deliver the names to the clerk, be sure to ask when you can expect to pick up the credentials.

➤ If you submitted names and have not been notified that the credentials are ready for pick-up by the date provided, call immediately. Don't wait until the day before election-day to inquire as by then it might be too late to rectify the problem.

➢ It is always a good idea to submit more names than you will actually need in the polling places. This will provide cover in the event that a volunteer that was assigned to check bingo names inside the polling place is sick or otherwise unable to volunteer on election-day. Submitting extra names to be credentialed will ensure that you will have other credentialed volunteers to send in their stead.

❖ Bingo runners, the volunteers who will drive to each poll every hour to collect the completed bingo sheets from the bingo checkers, may also need to have credentials since they will have to enter the poll on a somewhat regular basis. It is better to submit those names and obtain credentials even if no one will be checking their credentials on election-day.

❖ Media Specialist is another volunteer that may need a credential, not from town hall, but rather from the candidate. Many press outlets will not accept advertisements or reserve advertisement space unless they are certain that the person claiming to represent your campaign actually does.

➢ Usually a letter signed by the candidate introducing the volunteer as your media specialist will suffice. It may be necessary to call some of the media outlets to determine exactly what they will accept from you to enable them to work with your assigned media specialist.

➢ Either forward a copy of credentials by email to every media outlet you will be utilizing or provide several copies to the media specialist, each copy with an original signature, for distribution as needed. It is very frustrating to be working against a submission deadline only to be rejected at the last minute because of a lack of proper credentials.

Some political jurisdictions are very unforgiving when it comes to requiring volunteers to show proper credentials before entering the polling place. Some jurisdictions are lax in that regard and others may not even have a credentialing process. But for those areas where a lack of proper credentialing can be used to prevent your volunteers from entering the polling place, assuring compliance with the credentialing requirements is an absolute necessity. Don't risk the success of your campaign efforts by failing to follow a few simple rules.

Chapter 9
Specific Campaign Activities

There are several customary events that most campaigns take advantage of. They range from the ordinary to the necessary in terms of importance and they generally carry no cost to execute, making them affordable to every campaign. Here is a listing of the more important events:

What All Voters Want

Many candidates claim that voters are complex. Voters are people and to the extent that people are complex, I guess voters are as well. However, it is not that difficult to know what voters want. All voters want pretty much the same thing from a politician. They want their elected officials to be trustworthy, honest, hardworking, available, caring, innovative and creative. You are a voter, isn't that what you want?

I believe, rather that it is the politician that is complex. So often I hear how a politician is aggravated by the 2:00, Saturday morning phone call from an aggrieved citizen who was abruptly awakened by the disturbance at the local pub as the crowd was disbursing at closing time. Sure, it may have been more prudent for the resident to call the police to lodge the complaint, or to call the elected official at a more reasonable hour, but that is not how many residents react, especially if the problem has been ongoing and little or nothing has been done to alleviate the resident's concerns. A public official is not elected to get aggravated. He/she is elected to serve the public and respond to the problems that plague the neighborhood. If you do not want to do either, why run for office in the first place?

This is why I believe that it is the politician that is complex. If you don't want to receive that phone call, don't run for office! If you don't want a voter complaining to you about the condition of the roads, about their street not being plowed within 1 hour of the snow storm ending, about their child not being eligible to ride the bus to school, or the recyclables being mixed with the solid waste by an uncaring trash hauler, or any other issue that you might find disruptive to your quiet life, then don't run for office. Generally speaking, residents will only call their elected official when they are aggravated with a particular situation and frustrated by the lack of address by the governing body. When that happens, the call is often times made right there on the spot, regardless of the time of day or night.

My philosophy and approach to my constituent's concerns was simply this: If an issue is important enough to a constituent to warrant a 2:00 A.M. phone call to me, then I better take the issue seriously regardless of how frivolous I believe it is or how inconvenient it is for me to take the call. I believe that attitude is the precise reason that, once elected, I never lost a re-election campaign.

If you are going to be aggravated by issues that you think are irrelevant, don't run for office.

In my opinion, the only thing you need to do to get re-elected every time you run for office is to be honest, caring, passionate, trustworthy, hardworking, innovative and available. In short, be the kind of politician that every voter wants. If you can't be all of those things most of the time, then save yourself a lot of headaches and don't run for office.

However, before you can prove to the voters that you ARE that kind of politician, you need to be elected. The following is a list of the major activities that your campaign should undertake in order for you to win your first election.

The Campaign Announcement

Some candidates have very elaborate affairs in a fancy hall with a three piece band, food, decorations, etc. These type events serve as both a formal announcement and a campaign rally at the same time. They are generally reserved for larger, statewide campaigns and can be costly. For a local race they are also not necessary. Some ideas more suitable for a local campaign announcement might include:

- ❖ Theme-oriented announcement – This was always my preferred type of announcement event. They can be held at an outdoor site of relevance in your district. At the time of my first successful campaign, a major issue confronting my district was the repair of a local damn that broke causing the water to drain from a river's retention pond. The pond itself had been created over 150 years earlier when an old mill was established in the area and had been all that generations of residents had ever know to exist there. Formerly water-front homes were now fronted on mud pits and eventually overgrown aquatic grasses. It was unsightly and odorous and was causing a rapid devaluation of the properties that were still being taxed as waterfront. The neighbors were particularly unhappy and the town's people in general were disappointed at the loss of a beautiful water resource. To many, it didn't matter how the repair might adversely impact the budget, it mattered only that the resource and property values were restored. I announced my candidacy in front of the broken dam vowing that I wouldn't rest until the dam was repaired and the town's water resource, the pond that my dad had once swum in as a boy, was restored. It made for a great photo op, cost nothing and attracted local press that included print media, radio and television, most of which probably would not have attended my announcement if it had been more conventional, less controversial in nature.

As a side note, the dam was repaired within two years and that is a long time in the minds of the residents who demanded swift action, I was sure to keep the neighbors to whom the repair mattered most apprised of each development with regular update flyers that I delivered to each home personally every 8-10 weeks along the way. The residents were both informed and reassured that I was working on the issue along with several other state and federal officials and that I had their backs.

❖ In lieu of any announcement event, you may choose to simply issue a press release advising the media that you are running and mentioning the issues you will be addressing. This is not the time to offer specific proposals. That will happen as the campaign progresses. Rather a simple listing of the issues is enough to provide a decent announcement release.

Press Releases – the Format of the Release

Press Releases offer another opportunity to deliver your message for free at election time. I always made it a practice to issue one release per week for the 8-10 week election cycle each addressing a different plank in my platform. If there were 8 planks, then I had enough issues to spread throughout the campaign season. If you have only 4 planks you can spread your releases out accordingly. On those weeks that you have no specific campaign issue to address, then simply issue a press release announcing your campaign committee appointments or a debate challenge to your opponent. Regardless of the subject of the release, don't let a single week of the campaign pass by without having a press release in the local newspaper.

❖ *Writing the Press Release* – All press releases should be written on your campaign letterhead and they should all be in a single style throughout the campaign. This will make it easier for the reporter to recognize a legitimate release submitted by your campaign and will make the release easily recognizable as yours. Your letterhead doesn't need to be fancy or expensive. Something crafted on your computer using a large attractive font style will do. Be sure to have your name, address, phone number (preferably the cell phone number), the email address and the website address. Don't be afraid to make it colorful so that it stands out to the reporters.

➢ *Headline* – The headline should contain the candidate's name and a relatively short description of what will be contained in the release. And it should be written in a large (16 font) bold print and be centered on the top of the page. A sample headline might look like this:

Smith Proposes City-wide Street Resurfacing Program

➢ *Sub-headline* - The sub-headline should also be in bold print but with a font size of 14. It too will be centered on the page and sit just below the headline. It should contain a short description of a major point in the release. *Be sure that everything in the headline and sub-headline is accurate and factual.* A sample sub-headline will look like this:

Candidate describes condition of the streets of Jonestown as the worst in the state and contends that many streets haven't been resurfaced in over 20 years.

➢ **Publication date** – Not all press releases are meant to be released immediately. Some are issued early so as to meet a publication deadline or because you want to be sure that the editor knows that you issued your release before another candidate addressed the same issue, but you want the reporter to hold off on printing the story. The next line of the release therefore will tell the reporter when you would like the press release to be reported. That is typically done by writing the release instructions on the next line of the press release and placing the instructions in 12-font, bold print, and setting it apart in parenthesis. For example;

(For Immediate Release)
or **(For Release on Tuesday July 7, 2015)**

Sometimes news is embargoed. That simply means that, although you have been given certain information, the source has asked that you not make it public until a certain date giving that person time to get their affairs in order. For example, the Department of Public Works may have provided you with a list of streets that it intends to pave and the order in which it intends to resurface them along with the dates of resurfacing. The Director of DPW asked that you hold off making a public announcement, however, until he/she has had a chance to brief the Mayor which he/she plans to do on Wednesday July 8th. You know that while the local newspaper is not released until Thursday July 9th, their deadline to send the paper to print is Wednesday. Releasing the information with a note of the embargo will allow the editor to include the article in the paper without placing the information on its website earlier than the embargo date ensuring that the DPW Director will be able to brief the Mayor before he reads it in the paper or on-line. The embargo is noted on the press release as follows:

Embargo – Information May Not Be Released Until Thursday July 9, 2015

> **Body of the release** – The body of the release should be written in 12 font type and set up in paragraph form. Most reporters want the release to be double spaced, but I have found 1.5 spaces to be adequate. Unless the release is addressing a major proposal, short is better. It is unlikely that routine press releases that are more than 1 to 1.5 pages will be printed, and if they are, they will be edited significantly with the reporter, rather than the candidate,

getting to choose which details remain and which are edited out.

✓   The release should always begin with the candidate's name and a statement of the issue. For example, *"John Smith, candidate for council district 4 said today that if elected he will make the resurfacing of streets one of his first priorities."*

✓   If the release is of a controversial nature, something reporters tend to prefer more than the mundane type of release then be sure to back up the facts you claim by citing sources. You may even want to include a copy of the report from which you gleaned the facts to save the reporter the time of having to fact check your information himself. For example, if you are claiming, as I did in the example above, that the condition of the streets are the worst in the state, then indicate where that information was derived. You might say, *"According to the street condition report issued on October 1, 2013 by the State Department of Transportation, Jonestown has the distinction of having the worst streets in the state based on condition. (see page 32 of the attached report)"*

✓   Next, you should explain why this issue is important to your constituents. You might write. *"Potholes are known to cause significant damage to motor vehicles. Even when the vehicle suffers no visible damage, the frame alignment is altered causing tires to wear out faster and significantly reducing the vehicle's gas mileage, costing residents a staggering amounts of money. Residents of Jonestown pay a significant amount of property tax and should expect that a fair* amount of that money will be spent to maintain their roads so as not to destroy the value of their vehicle or create unnecessary repairs and additional expenses due to reduced gas mileage."

✓ The body of the release should also explain what you propose to do to rectify the problem. The proposed solution should be specific and contain all the information of relevance and importance. For example, you might write, *"When elected to the town council,"* Smith said, *"I will ask the Department of Public Works to inventory every street in the town and create a priority list of those that need immediate attention. I will devote an amount of money to the budget sufficient to pave all those streets in the first two years of my term. Other streets will be assigned a number based on their condition and those streets will be paved during years 3 and 4 of my term of office. Therefore, before the end of my first term on the town council, every street in Jonestown will have been re-paved,"* Smith continued.

✓ Finally, indicate how you intend to pay for the road resurfacing program and the impact that it will have on taxes. You might write, *Smith concluded, "I know that this program is ambitious and will have a cost attached. I will aggressively seek Jonestown's share of federal and state funds available for this purpose. I will also devote 15% of the current DPW budget for road resurfacing and will allocate those funds formerly dedicated to the payout of claims against the town because of damage caused to the vehicles of both residents and non-residence alike. I believe that most will agree that those funds are much better* spent eliminating the problem than paying for the consequences of not addressing the issue."

➤ **Contact Information** - Always conclude the release by signing your name and including a contact name and number that the reporter can call for additional information. This sentence should always appear at the end of all your press releases, *"For additional information contact John Smith at 450-619-0345."* It is certainly permissible to include the media specialists name rather than the candidates name here if you choose to.

Pre-Election Day Ballots / Voting

Some states allow for in-person pre-election day voting. In those states, it may be important to establish the election-day activities for a significant period of time. That is very difficult to do when volunteers are such a precious commodity. In most states, however, pre-election day ballots are more traditionally known as absentee and/or shut-in ballots. Election law generally provides for voters who are not able to get to the polls on election-day for health reasons (*shut-in ballots*) or because they will physically be out of the state or country on election-day (*absentee ballots)* or because they are in the military (or family of those serving in the military *(UOCAVA voters),* an opportunity to receive and cast a ballot prior to election day. Some states allow for no-excuse absentee balloting as well. In many cases these individuals are allowed to have ballots delivered at an address other than their residence. There is an application process and there are very specific laws that govern ballot delivery and ballot delivery deadlines. Because these laws are so state or jurisdiction specific you will want to check the details at your local election board.

❖ Mail ballots

➢ Request blank mail ballot applications and carry them with you throughout campaign.

✓ Every candidate, while campaigning, meets voters who say, "I would love to support you but I will be on vacation on election-day or I am having surgery and will not be able to get to the polls." There is a reasonable certainty that if the voter is making this comment to you, he/she is one of your supporters. Do not allow that ballot to go uncast as long as the voter is willing, and legally allowed, to vote early.

✓ Offer the opportunity for them to vote by applying for the appropriate shut-in, absentee or UOCAVA ballot. Also be sure that they complete the application and return it to the appropriate election body (either the local board of canvassers or the state election board depending upon the rules of your specific political jurisdiction.

✓ Be sure to add their names to your "supporter list" and follow-up with them to ensure that their ballot was mailed and received by them and that they completed it and returned it in accordance with the instructions. If the voter should ask you for assistance be sure to follow all the laws that govern the provision of such assistance. Some states prohibit the candidate from personally assisting voters in the completion of mail ballots instead requiring bona-fide election officials to handle the task.

➤ Tracking mail ballot applications.

✓ Check with the town clerk's office to determine how many absentee, shut-in and UOCAVA ballots were issued in your district and get the list of names of who they were delivered to.

✓ Write a short letter to each of those voters asking for his/her vote and explaining why you deserve consideration. Enclose a brochure and explain how grateful you will be for his/her favorable consideration.

✓ Chances are you might be the only candidate to take the time to write to them. If so, you will stand a reasonably good chance of getting their vote. Even if the competition is stiff, by writing and asking for it, you increase your chances of getting the vote.

Many local elections have been decided by just a few votes and I have seen some election-day voting end in a tie vote. If your race is too close to call when all machine ballots are tallied, you will be very grateful to know that you took the time to "campaign" to those voters that applied for, received and voted on a mail ballot.

Debates

Unless you are an incumbent running against a complete unknown, you will probably want to challenge your opponent to a debate or a series of debates. If you are confident of the issues and your ability to discuss them in such a forum, then a debate is a wonderful way to address the issues, gain name recognition and impress voters all at the same time. It is also a time when you can hold your opponent publicly accountable for any misdeeds thereby potentially altering the discourse of the campaign.

❖ For these reasons, an incumbent will probably not want to accept the debate challenge. Press the issue with your opponent and don't let him/her off the hook quite so easily. Let the press know that you are available to debate at your opponent's convenience and how terrible it would be to deny the public the opportunity to hear the candidates explain their position on the issues that are so vital to their future and the future direction of the town.

❖ Repeat the challenge two or three times throughout the campaign until your opponent agrees to discuss the issues with you in a public forum that will enable the voter to compare each of you side-by-side or declines the invitation. If he/she continues to refuse, frame the discussion by saying that the fact that the opponent is not dedicated to transparency as indicated by refusing to debate during the campaign, is reason enough to assume that he/she will continue to operate under the cover of darkness if elected. This may just become an overriding issue of the campaign making all of his other proposals seem shallow by comparison.

Door – to - Door Canvassing and Voter Scoring

Local campaigns in smaller districts provide the unique opportunity of meeting the voters by walking to every door in your district. If it is manageable, you may want to consider walking to every door twice, at least in your first campaign. There is no more personal way to introduce yourself to the voters that will make the voter feel most comfortable than meeting him/her at his/her home. Take advantage of every day of dry weather by canvassing the district in this fashion, but be sure that you are prepared to both express yourself without notes and respond to questions from the heart. This will require that you have a total command of the issues of importance to the voters that you will be meeting. Take the time to have a campaign person quiz you by asking you questions that a voter might ask so that you will not be caught off guard by a voter. Practice the answers so that you will know how you want to answer each question in a way that is polite, non-confrontational and confident. A voter will not appreciate a timid response, an evasive response, or a candidate that fumbles with the response.

- ❖ **Walking door to door/canvassing**
  - ➢ The first time you campaign at the voter's home introduce yourself, tell them what office you are running for and give them a copy of your brochure. Ask them to review it and ask them if it would be ok to stop back further along in the campaign to answer any questions they may have about you or your candidacy. Ask if any other voters are at home that you might be able to say hello to and/or that might need to register to vote. After all, you want to take advantage of this opportunity to meet and register as many people as possible. Tell the voter that you would be grateful for their support if they like what you are proposing in your brochure.

    NOTE: always carry voter registration cards with you so that you can register new voters on the spot if you meet someone who is not registered. Be sure that candidates are allowed to act as a registration agent in your political jurisdiction. If not, try to have a registration agent walk with you or take the person's name and phone number so your registration agent can contact them.

➢ If they offer immediate support, ask if it would be OK to put a lawn sign in their front yard. If they agree, put it up as soon as you get back to your car. If they refuse tell them you understand and that you hope to gain their confidence throughout the course of the campaign.

➢ Keep track of who you meet by underlining their name on your "walking sheets." Also, be sure to rank each voter you meet by circling one of the 1-5 numbers next to the voter's name in blue ink after you have left their property. *NOTE: for additional information refer to the section on door-to-door canvassing chapter 7*

➢ If you are able to make a second visit to the same home later in the campaign, reintroduce yourself and remind the voter what office you are running for while handling the voter a different piece of literature than the one you distributed on your first visit.

➢ If you are speaking with the same voter (the name underlined from the first visit) refer to him/her by the last name (Mr. or Mrs. Smith) and ask if they have had a chance to read about you and if they have any questions either about you or what you are proposing to do. When the conversation ends, politely ask again for the vote, and whether there might be any other voters at home that you could say hello to.

➢ If they offer support, ask permission to place a small lawn sign on their front lawn. Thank them for their time (and/or support) and mark your walking sheet in a different color (red) ink after you leave their property. The different ink colors will enable you to identify when you spoke to them later on if that information becomes important to you.

➢   If no one is home when you arrive at the door, it does not have to be a wasted stop. Leave a brochure in the door handle or in the screen door if there is one. Many candidates will write a "Sorry I missed you" message on the brochure before leaving it in the door. I always preferred a longer message that actually said something to the voter. You won't want to spend time writing a long message while standing at the door, however, so you will need to prepare those brochures at home prior to starting your walking tour. One good idea is to type a ¼ page message

NOTE: Type four messages to a page, make several hundred copies and then cut them into ¼ page messages. In my experience about 50% of the homes that I walked to were not answered. Sometimes there was simply no one home. At other times I could tell someone was home, they simply didn't want to be bothered at that particular time. If you run out of prepared brochures early in your walk, you will find yourself wasting a lot of quality walking time writing messages on brochures rather than meeting voters. The message could read, "I'm sorry that I was not able to discuss my candidacy for town council with you. I have so many ideas that I wanted to discuss and I am excited to get your perspective of the town's needs. I hope to walk your neighborhood again before the end of the campaign. In the meantime, please review my brochure. If you have any questions about me, my candidacy and/or my proposals to improve the quality of life for the residents of our town, please do not hesitate to contact me at (list your phone number here). I really want your vote, but I want to earn it. Thank you for taking the time to read about me. (Sign your name in blue ink so that they will see it is an original signature.)

This message gives the voter an idea of your commitment and will make you stand out among all the other candidates that leave brochures in their door.

❖ **The Tote Board**
On election night you will want to display a large tote board in your headquarters showing the vote tally and displaying the results of the election for all assembled to see. A volunteer should be assigned this task and given instructions on how to make it.

➤ The tote board should be drawn on a 3' X 5' sheet of foam core mount.

➤ Your name and the names of all your opponents should be written in large letters in a vertical column along the far left side of the board leaving sufficient space between names so as to allow you to write large enough so people in the back of the room will be able to read it.

➤ Across the top of the board you should list all the precinct numbers (IE: 4A, 4B, 4C, etc.) followed by a column with the word "total" written in it.

➤ Draw a line under each precinct number and under the word "total" to align with the name of each candidate listed.

➢ The night before election, hang the tote board on the wall in front of the room in such a manner that a volunteer will be able to write the tally from each precinct as they are called into headquarters by the poll checker. Essentially, the board will need to be against a wall or some other hard surface and not swinging free-style from the ceiling.

While none of the aforementioned activities cost any money, they all give you an opportunity to define yourself and your message. That is something you always want to do in a campaign. Never let the opponent define you or drive the debate. Don't create a situation where you are forced to respond to your opponent's claims. It is much more advantageous to frame the message and define the campaign issues yourself.

Technology

Finally, if money is more available to you than manpower, there are campaign and get-out-the-vote services that you can take advantage of. Advances have made some amazing technologies available to candidates, technology that can replace hundreds of hours of volunteer activities. Here are a few ideas:

❖ *Robo-calls* – Have you ever received one of those annoying automated business phone calls? They always seem to come at the least opportune time. Well now they are available to campaigners as well. Your entire district can receive a phone call with a prerecorded message from you and in your voice. The messages can vary and can be placed for as little as 2 cents each.

➢ If you asked volunteers to call everyone in a voting district of 1,500 households, it could take them tens of hours to complete the task. With Robo-calling technology, the task can be completed in a few short minutes and everyone will receive a personal message from you reminding them to vote for you on election-day.

➢   As I noted at the outset however, these calls can be annoying so if you make use of the technology, keep the message short – 10 or 15 seconds at most. Speak in an upbeat, optimistic voice but explain the urgency of the election for the town, and don't forget to ask for the vote!

❖   *Mail Services* – There are services that will affix your mail labels to an envelope, fold, stuff, seal, and mail them all for just pennies apiece. Again, this will save many hours of volunteer time, but you will have to pay for the service.

❖   *Polling Services* – Many companies will conduct telephone surveys or polls for you. Depending upon the scientific nature of the poll, it can become an expensive and involved proposition. However some of the stripped down versions that don't involve an analysis of trends and issues, but rather simply gauge whether the person being called is registered to vote, likely to vote in the election, and who they are likely to support given a list of names, can be purchased at more affordable prices.

❖   *Phone banking Services* – Some companies offer a complete phone bank that you can use on election-day if volunteers are unavailable for that purpose. However, making use of a phone bank service may negate your ability to utilize a bingo system which I believe is a critical function for the campaign.

➢ There is even predictive dialing software downloads that can be purchased to give your volunteers the ability to make outbound calls from the comfort of their own homes rather than having to spend time on election-day at the headquarters.

➢ Again, I'm not a big fan of this because I prefer to monitor the calls in the event of an issue, or to ensure that the calls are actually being made, but it is nice to know that such technology is available to those that have no other option.

Chapter 10
Getting Press Coverage

When your campaign is struggling to raise money, alternative methods of attracting press coverage are not only highly desirable, but a practical necessity. Press coverage is free but is not always easy to come by. There are a great many campaigns throughout the state, and many of those candidates are probably running for offices considered more press worthy than the local office that you are seeking. So with all the competition, how will you attract consistent free press coverage? With a little creative thinking, even your campaign for a school committee or town council seat can earn you significant press coverage, but you have to know what reporters are looking for and then be willing to offer it.

What All Reporters Want

In chapter 9 we discussed the structure of the press release; the headline, sub-headline, hook, and other elements of design. In this chapter we will review the details of writing the release in a style that will vastly improve the odds that it will generate press coverage far beyond what you might think possible in a campaign for a local office.

Any reporter with a modicum of ambition and self-respect will chase a story that will land him/her on the paper's front-page. Not all stories meritorious of front-page placement, however, will wind up on the front page of the newspaper because other events that occur, events that are beyond your control, may override your story in the eyes of the editors. But that doesn't mean the story does not have front page potential. You may have just been a victim of bad timing.

Reporters also look for scoops and exclusives, that is, a story that no other news outlet has - and, reporters love controversy, especially salacious stories or stories about political corruption. Provide news of this type to a reporter and you will certainly receive a fair amount of press coverage. There are several ways you can pique a reporter's interest in your story. Here are a few ideas.

Creating the News Story

Not all news is created equal. Some news is earth shattering while other news is relatively meaningless to a reporter. The trick is attracting reporters to your stories. This objective can be accomplished in a couple of ways.

❖ Adding certain elements to your release will help ensure good media coverage of your proposals. The elements of emotion, uniqueness, excitement, controversy, and conflict helps sell newspapers and that is exactly what every newspaper publisher, and consequently, reporter, wants to do.

❖   It is not hard to fill your press release with one or more of these elements. An emotion-filled story rather than a mundane candidate statement will pique a reporter's interest, but that sentiment has to be conveyed in the first couple of sentences of the release.

❖   For example, if you are a candidate for town council and you are proposing a street repaving program, you have a few options available to you in the promotion of your proposal. One option might land you a press release in the next edition of the paper, while another might motivate the reporter to pursue the candidate with additional questions and perhaps some photographs. Done the right way, a press release submitted by a candidate for local office may even attract television news coverage.

❖   Take a look at the opening paragraph of this one-page press release and decide for yourself which version is likely to attract the best press coverage.

➢   **Option #1**
    John Smith, candidate for town council, Jonestown district 4, announced today that when elected, he will inventory the town's streets for the purpose of prioritizing a street paving program that he intends to undertake within the first 100 days of his term of office.

While this is a worthwhile undertaking for any council candidate, there is nothing here that would cause the news reporter to do anything except print part or maybe all of the release submitted.

> ➢ *Option #2*
> *John Smith, candidate for town council, Jonestown district 4, noted that the deplorable condition of the town's streets is costing the town over $30,000 each year in claims paid to residents who have suffered extraordinary damage to their vehicles as a result of the many potholes. This cost, Smith contends, could be easily averted by instituting a comprehensive street paving program and that is just what he will do when elected. Jane taxpayer said that her "car repair bill exceeded $300 as a result of damage when she drove into a pothole too large to avoid on Dyer Avenue last week....*

This release may prompt the reporter to investigate the number of pothole-related claims that have been paid out by the town as well as the total cost of paying those claims. The reporter may even contact the candidate and/or the resident for additional comment. I also believe that a television reporter would find an interview with the resident holding the car repair bill on location at the pothole an irresistible story!

> ➢ *Option #3*
> *John Smith, candidate for town council, Jonestown district 4 announced today that upon taking office he will assess the condition of local roads, prioritize the streets in order of greatest need of repair and immediately commence a comprehensive road repaving initiative. Smith explained that the town spends significant amounts of money paying claims to residents whose vehicles suffered serious damage with routine travel along our town's deplorable streets.*

One resident, 67-year old Mary Johnson, while traveling only 25 miles per hour on a road less than ½ mile from her home, broke her front axil after hitting what she described as a "pothole large enough to swallow my front left tire."

The pothole has still not been repaired by town workers and tomorrow morning at 10:00 A.M. candidate Smith and Mary Johnson will meet at the site with some cold patch in an effort to prevent further damage or personal injury by filling in the pothole themselves.

Option #1 is OK and may get you a story somewhere within the local weekly newspaper. Option #2 is more likely to generate interest from the daily newspaper and generate some television coverage. Option #3 will more than likely attract reporters from the local weekly and the statewide daily newspapers, as well as radio and television reporters all hoping to catch a glimpse of 67-year old Mary and the candidate shoveling cold patch into the pothole that the town has ignored even after paying out a significant damage claim to Mary several months ago.

This story has now turned into a possible series with various reporters following different angles to the story. Some reporters may track down other "victims" of road damage. Others may run around town looking for the streets in deplorable condition and interviewing residents who live on those streets hoping for some disparaging comments about the council's leadership. Each of these stories will feature you and your proposal at the time when your press release is originally issued and probably a second time when the town is finally embarrassed into taking corrective action.

❖ Regardless of how far the story goes, one thing is clear, you have just gotten thousands of dollars-worth of press coverage for the very affordable price of "free!" The concept of each of the three options presented is basically the same. The approach to reporting the concept is what changed. A little out of the box thinking can go a long way in promoting your ideas with thousands of dollars of free press coverage.

Reporters Need News

Don't forget that reporters are in constant need of fresh news and they need to respond to those people who can create news for them. Don't be afraid, in every press release that you write, to look for the angle that will turn your proposal into the exact type of story the reporter has been dreaming of. The subject matter is sometimes far less important when it comes to news coverage than is the manner in which the subject is presented. Be sure that every press release you issue has the elements that will excite the reporter into action.

Chapter 11
The Bingo System – Part I

BINGO

12	25	41	51	63
3	30	37	54	66
7	21	FREE	56	74
1	26	35	50	69
10	17	45	47	64

Preparing the Bingo System

The bingo system is a device used over the course of your campaign to identify the pool of potential voters, track the level of potential support for your candidacy (or that of your opponent,) and ensure that those identified as your supporters actually get to the polls to cast their ballot on election-day. All of this is intended to provide you with a measurement of your level of success throughout election-day so that you can most efficiently allocate resources to maximize your chances of success. While it sounds extremely complex, it is actually not an overly complicated system to employ, but it is labor intensive and requires many volunteers, particularly on election-day, to execute. Here's how it works:

❖ *Acquisition of the voting lists*

➢ You must acquire an accurate and up to date voter list. These are generally available for purchase at the local board of canvassers, Secretary of State's office or your state board of elections. It is generally not too expensive to purchase a complete voter list for a local race and depending on size may be well under $100.

➢ You will probably not be able to acquire the most up to date list until after the voter registration deadline has passed in those states that require registration prior to voting. Some states provide a preliminary list and then issue a supplement containing the names of new registrants shortly after the registration deadline. All of this information will be available at your local board of canvassers.

➢ Almost all poll books list the names of the voters in alphabetical order of the voter's last name followed by the voter's address.

❖ *Preparation of the voting lists*

➢ Once you have obtained the voting lists, instruct volunteers to number each name on the list beginning with the number one at the start of every new letter. For example, let's assume that the district in which you are running for council is called council district 1 and that within council district 1 there are 6 polling locations labeled district 1A, 1B, 1C, 1D 1E and 1F. Each polling place will more than likely have a separate voting list.

NOTE: if your district employs the use of an electronic poll book each district may be provided with the complete voting list for the entire town but the names may be distinguishable by voting district.

The volunteer will begin with poll book 1A and start with the names that begin with the letter "A." Consequently, if there are 40 names each beginning with the letter A, they will be numbered 1-40 and will be referred to as A1, A2, A3, etc. The volunteer will then move on to the letter B, then the letter C and so on until the numbering of the book is complete. That process will be repeated for voting precinct books 1B through 1F. If you have to incorporate the names of new registrants from a supplemental voting list, those names can be labeled SA1, SA2, SA3, etc.

❖ **Duplicate the list after the bingo numbering process is completed**

➢ Once all the names of each precinct's voting book are numbered, copy the voting list so that there are two identical sets of numbered "bingo'd poll books."

➢ One of the sets will be kept intact, while each individual page of the second set will be separated from the book and hung on the wall sequentially prior to election-day.

✓ You will probably have several rows of pages and may even have several walls papered.

✓ No book should be hung higher than the about 5' from the floor enabling a volunteer of average height to easily read the top name and highlight or cross out a name as required.

✓ The name of any voter identified as a 1 or 2 by the candidate on the walking sheets completed during the door-to-door canvassing should be highlighted with a yellow marker on both copies of the voting books. In small letters next to the voter's name write the letters "WS" which stands for "walking sheets." This will be used later to let the election-day bingo volunteer know how this voter was identified as a supporter.

➢ Throughout the course of the campaign, but prior to election-day eve every volunteer, friend or relative of the candidate must also review this list very carefully identifying anyone on the list that the reviewer knows is supporting the candidate. The reviewer will highlight the name of every voter that he/she is confident will support the candidate and place his/her initials next to the name that he/she highlighted.

NOTE: My rule was always to tell the volunteers to only highlight the name of a person that you know so well or trust so much that they will vote for the candidate of your choice simply because you are asking them to do so. If you have 30 volunteers and each can identify only 10 such people (generally parents, children, siblings, etc,) that is a solid 300 votes that you can count on, easily enough to sway a local election.

✓ Hopefully, by election-day there will be enough highlighted names to coincide with the number of votes that you have determined to be required for victory. *(Refer to the section on "planning for victory" at the end of chapter 6.)*

✓ If there are not a sufficient number of voters identified by volunteers and the walking sheets to ensure victory, then you may have to resort to a closer scrutiny of the "3s" on the walking sheets to better determine if they are likely to support your candidacy.

❖ *Preparing the polling place bingo sheets*

➢ Preparing the voting lists represents only part of the bingo system. The other part is equally important. Volunteers must design the polling place bingo sheets.

✓ The best design fits on an 8.5 X 11 piece of plain copy paper drawn with 26 boxes of equal size resembling a calendar.

✓ In the upper right corner of each box make a smaller box, writing in each box a different letter of the alphabet in order from A to Z.

✓ Draw a line at top left side of the form labeled "polling Place and district" and a second line at the top right of the form labeled "time." Draw a third line at the bottom of the form labeled "checker's signature."

✓ Assemble packets by stapling 15 of these blank forms together. Every volunteer that will work as a bingo checker inside the polling place on election-day will be provided with one packet of these forms, at least enough so as to enable the volunteer to record information on a new form beginning at each new hour of election-day. For example, if the polls open at 7:00 a.m. and close at 9:00 p.m., the first form will read "*7:00 a.m. to 8:00 a.m.*" The second form will be read "*8:00 a.m. to 9:00 a.m.*" and so on until the last form that will read "*8:00 pm. to 9:00 p.m.*" The forms should be pre-filled by volunteers, copied, and then stapled together forming the 15 page package.

NOTE: filling in the time information before copying the forms will save the time of having to label the packets for the several different polling locations individually.

❖ **Assigning the Packets to the volunteer poll checkers**

➢ While there may be several bingo checkers assigned to each polling location on election-day, only one (or two if the checkers will be working in pairs) will be assigned to open the poll at 7:00 A.M. That is the bingo checker that should receive the "poll kit," on the eve of election-day.

✓ The "poll kit" contains all the material the bingo checker will need to perform his/her function on election-day. These materials include:

▪ The 15-page package of bingo forms

▪ Two sharpened pencils with erasers

- The bingo'd voter list for the appropriate voting precinct

- Credentials for each checker assigned at the particular polling location on election-day

  NOTE: not all political jurisdictions require the credentialing of poll workers. This is something that needs to be determined prior to election-day as described in chapter 8.

- The tally sheet for the final results to be taken at the close of the polls. Generally the bingo worker who is working the last shift will remain in the polling place to get the results from that precinct and call the result into headquarters. The tally sheet should include the number that the volunteer is to call to relay the polling location's vote result.

- The volunteer bingo checker that closes the poll should be instructed to pack all the material back in the box and return it to headquarters at the end of the night after the results are taken from that polling location.

Section III

Election Day Activities
Working the Plan

Chapter 12
The Bingo System – Part II

Working the Bingo System

The bingo system described in this book is so accurate a tool that during a re-election campaign for a sitting Speaker of the House, our team of "North Providence Assassins," as we were later dubbed, was able to predict the result of the race hours before the polls closed, to within $1/10^{th}$ of 1 percent of the actual vote tally. That kind of accuracy, however, is dependent upon the accurate detail that goes into working the system from the outset. When it comes to employing a successful bingo system, accuracy is required during every step of the process. From the candidate recording accurate "support/no support" rankings during the door to door canvassing, to volunteers identifying their own known supporters of your candidacy, to the checking at the polls, to the retrieval of the forms by the runner and the get-out-the-vote (GOTV) phone calls made from the headquarters, if any step is done haphazardly, the result will be imperfect and misleading. The checkers role at the polling place is no less critical as the recording of a wrong name, or the placement of the voter's corresponding bingo number in the wrong box, will result in bad information back at headquarters. The following is a step by step instruction of the checker's function on election-day:

❖ *Receiving the voter's name*

➢ As each voter enters the polling place he/she must identify him/herself and sign a form in order to receive a ballot. While this is happening the municipal poll worker will yell out the name of the voter so that the bingo checker can hear it. If the reading of the name is unclear, or if there are two people with the same or a similar name, further identified as a Jr., or with a different address, the municipal poll worker will note that. If he/she doesn't, then the checker must ask the municipal poll worker for clarification. The volunteer is not allowed, however, to disrupt official poll proceedings. Therefore, if it is very busy and there is a line forming, the checker may have to make a written note of the question and ask it at a time when there is not a line of people waiting to vote. Regardless of when the issue is clarified, it must be clarified. It is of critical importance to the success of the bingo system that the checker receives and records the correct information.

➢ Once it is clear who has just voted, the checker will look up that voter's name on his corresponding voting list.

➢ Once the bingo checker has located the proper voter's name, he/she will then cross the voter's name off the voting list, signifying that the person has now voted, and proceed to record the bingo number in the appropriate box on the bingo sheet. For example, if John J. Smith walks into the poll and is given a ballot, the municipal poll worker will yell, "JOHN J. SMITH" in a clear and loud voice. The bingo checker will flip the voting list to the page with the names beginning with the letter "S" and visually scroll down the list until the name "SMITH, John J." is located.

NOTE: If there is more than one John J. Smith, the volunteer should ask the municipal poll worker for an address or other distinguishing characteristic.

The correct name is then crossed off the voting list and the corresponding bingo number assigned to that name is recorded on the bingo sheet. At the end of each hour a bingo runner will come into the poll, and collect the bingo sheet for the current hour.

❖ *The role of the bingo poll runner*

➢ Once each hour the bingo runner will collect the hourly bingo sheet from each polling place in the district and promptly return the hourly sheets from all polling locations to headquarters.

✓ The bingo runner can also be used to deliver food and drinks to the bingo checkers and visibility volunteers working outside each polling place.

✓ The runner should have a cooler filled with cold drinks in the trunk of his/her car and distribute the drinks to those that need them throughout the day.

✓ Be mindful that some volunteers will be working through breakfast, lunch and/or dinner and may need food once or more than once throughout the day. If you want the volunteer to continue working, you will need to feed them.

❖ *The bingo coordinator and the bingo headquarters volunteers*

➢ Once back at headquarters, the bingo coordinator will receive the hourly bingo sheets and assign them to volunteers for processing.

➢ The coordinator must be sure to check the polling precinct identification on the bingo sheet and ensure that the volunteer is matching the bingo numbers on the sheet against the corresponding number on the correct precinct voting list. By now it should be clear why one set of voting books is numbered and then copied creating a second identical book rather than numbering two different sets of voting books in the original. By copying the one numbered set, any mistake resulting from the inaccurate numbering of the names will be repeated in the second book meaning that when that number is recorded at the polling place, it will correspond to the same voter's name in the book back at headquarters.

✓ Remember, each precinct will have many of the same numbers, but an "S32" on the bingo sheet from district 1A will represent a different voter than the "S32" on the bingo sheet from district 1B, 1C, etc.

➢ In the confusion that can be generated on this hectic day, it will be easy to cross reference the bingo sheet with the wrong voting list resulting in two errors that could prove fatal to the bingo results. It cannot be overstated that accuracy is critical if the bingo system is to work effectively.

➢ Those volunteers will locate each number on the bingo list and identify the voter's name by finding the corresponding number on the voting list hanging on the wall. This should be done under the watchful eye of the bingo coordinator to verify that the bingo sheet numbers are being applied to the right voting list.

➢ The volunteer will then cross off that voter's name *in pencil* signifying that his/her vote has been cast.

❖ *Late day reaction to the bingo system results*

➢ As the day progresses, the bingo coordinator will be able to see at a glance how many people cast ballots from each precinct and how many of those voters were expected to cast ballots for you.

➢ This information will provide the candidate with an hourly running "score" of the election result. The only unknown quantity will be any voter who was recorded on the walking sheets as a "3." While you may not know with certainty who the #3 voted for, you will know at what point of the campaign you peaked. If your campaign momentum was rising or peaking on the last couple of days of the campaign, then chances are good that those undecided voters are breaking in your favor.

➤ Hopefully, the majority of names being crossed off the headquarters voting list were highlighted in yellow indicating that they were likely to have voted for you. However, if you notice that at about 2-3 hours before the polls are scheduled to close a substantial number of voters highlighted in yellow have not yet voted, then some additional volunteers should be brought back to headquarters to make reminder calls to those voters.

➤ This is also the point of the campaign where those little initials that each volunteer wrote next to the name that he/she highlighted on the voting books hanging on the wall will come in handy. The volunteer that identified the voter as a supporter is the one that should call the voter and ask him/her to go vote.

❖ *The candidate's election-day role in bingo system implementation*

➤ Even the candidate should leave the polls at this point and return to headquarters to make phone calls to known supporters who have not yet voted.

➤ Nothing is more compelling to one of your supporters than receiving a last minute plea from the candidate to get out and vote in support of his efforts.
   ✓ Call the supporter and say, *"Hi John. Our records indicate that you haven't voted yet. This race is very close and could well be decided by just a few votes either way. We've worked so very hard to get to this point, it would be a shame to lose by 10 or 20 votes. If*

there is any way that you can make it to the polls before 9:00 p.m. (or whatever time the polls close in your area) I would be forever grateful. If you have other family members supporting me that also haven't voted, please see if they can go with you now. Can I count on you? Thank you so much."

To recap, the bingo system is something that you work on from the very first day of the campaign until the very last. The goal is to identify supporters, track those supporters that voted, and call those that haven't in a concerted effort to get them out to vote. If you identify enough voters to win the election, based upon historical voter turnout data, and ensure that nearly 100% of those voters identified go to the polls on election-day, you will have done all you could have done to run an effective campaign.

If you do that, and do it right, you will be victorious. It's that simple!

Chapter 13
Volunteers Outside the Polling Place

There are a plethora of activities taking place at the headquarters on election-day by a number of volunteers. They are working the bingo system, making phone calls, providing rides to the polls, delivering food to volunteer poll workers, and tending to every minor and major crisis that arises throughout the day. Meanwhile, there is another group of volunteers scattered throughout the district manning the polling places. We have discussed the bingo checkers in the previous chapter. However, we have not yet discussed the other off-site volunteers that are working so tirelessly in the field. These include:

❖ *The number of bingo runners that might be required*

➤ Bingo runners will be travelling between polling places and to and from headquarters all day. The number of polling places open in your district, and the distance between them will determine the number of bingo runners you will need. If one runner can make it from headquarters to all of the polls and back to headquarters in an hour, then only one will be needed.

➢ Keep in mind that the traffic around town may be heavier at the morning and afternoon rush hours, at lunchtime and when school gets out, than it will be at the other times of the day.

➢ In addition, you will need to be delivering food at various times too and that will slow the runner down. Take these factors into account when determining how many runners you will need.

❖ *Outside poll workers – visibility*

➢ The volunteers working outside the polling places will also have needs. In addition to food and drink, they will need a sufficient supply of give-a-way items to last the day. Someone, generally the runner(s) will have the responsibility of checking each hour to be sure their needs are met.

➢ If you have made a decision to not provide a give-a-way item to voters as they approach the polling place then the volunteer will hold one of the candidates signs and smile at or greet the voter as he approaches the poll.

➢ A typical greeting might sound like this, *"Good morning. Please consider voting for John Smith for council today."*

✓ Most voters are polite and will say an encouraging word. Others will ignore you and just walk past. Others still will ignore your gesture and approach the volunteer working for your opponent and strike up a conversation.

✓ These tell-tale signs will give the visibility volunteer a pretty good idea of how the vote is going in that polling place. This information should be reported to the runner each hour so the information can be relayed to headquarters.

✓ The voter's behavior can also be upsetting to a volunteer that is not accustomed to the rumble tumble antics of politics. Despite being upset, the volunteer must remain calm at all times and never, never, never say or do anything that might be considered confrontational to the voter. Some voters may even try to instigate a situation or harass the volunteer by saying disparaging things about the candidate he is supporting. The visibility volunteer, as is the case with all volunteers that represent you in your absence, MUST resist any temptation to retaliate verbally or otherwise. It is better to leave for a few minutes until the voter has left the area, than to engage the voter in any way.

❖ *Legal Counsel*

➤ Every state has laws that govern the conduct of visibility volunteers although those volunteers may be known by various titles in different states.

✓ Some laws govern the distance a volunteer may stand from the entrance to the polling place. If the visibility volunteer encroaches upon the prohibited space, he may be removed by police following up on the complaint of a voter or another candidate.

✓ It is important to check all the laws, rules and regulations that apply to volunteer poll workers. The volunteer should be given proper instructions prior to being dispatched to the polling place and he/she should be provided with a copy of the relevant laws to refer to if a question should arise.

✓ Many times the opposition will try to intimidate your volunteers, especially if they are very effective at their job, and hope that they will leave the polling place, leaving you with no coverage at that poll for a part of the day. If that happens, your volunteer should politely inform the intimidator that he/she (the volunteer) is in compliance with all the applicable laws. Do not leave, simply move further away and continue to greet voters, but contact the headquarters coordinator and inform him of the situation. The coordinator will contact legal counsel and dispatch him/her to the polling place to rectify the problem.

➢ The legal counsel may not be able to remain at headquarters all day, but should be available to deal with emergency situations such as the one described above.

➢ The legal counsel will also play a critical role at the end of the day when the votes are being tallied.

   ✓ If the race is very close, he may want to file a motion to impound the voting machines (or the memory units) to ensure that they are not tampered with until the state board of elections is able to exact a recount.

   ✓ The laws governing any activities in this regard are technical and vary widely from political jurisdiction to political jurisdiction. Be sure that your legal counsel familiarizes him/herself with all the relevant election laws prior to election-day so that appropriate action can be taken immediately upon being informed of the problem.

➢ There may be any number of legal issues that arise during the course of election-day and night. The legal counsel should try to anticipate the type of things that could occur and develop a strategy for dealing with each one. Different strategies may have to be developed depending upon the time of day/night that the problems occurs. Be ready for all eventualities.

   ✓ Potential legal issues include:
      • Placement of visibility volunteers.
      • Material being distributed.
      • Intimidation of volunteers.
      • Failure to allow credentialed volunteers into the polls.
      • Requests for recounts – impounding of voting equipment.
      • Illegal campaigning inside the polling place.

- Wrong ballots at the polling place.
- The evacuation of a poll during voting due to an emergency.
- A national disaster or terrorist threat at the polls.

❖ *Drivers*

➢ Inevitably there are voters that will call at the last minute asking for a ride to the polls. Most voters don't even think of how they will get to the polling place until the day of election. It is always best to have one or two passenger vans available to you on election-day, but if you don't have a volunteer that owns a passenger van or you don't know the owner of a car dealership that can donate one for the day, then use the largest, most comfortable car you have available.

➢ If you do have the use of a van or another vehicle that has a high step, be sure the driver has a step stool on board for elderly or physically impaired voters to use.

➢ The outside of the vehicle should be decorated with the candidates signs securely taped to the side doors or windows. There should also be a sign or sticker on the interior of the vehicle positioned in such a way that the voter must stare at it during the entire ride.

➢ When the driver reaches the voter's door he/she should open the car door, assist the voter in, and say, *"Thank you for calling John Smith for Council headquarters for a ride today. We would certainly appreciate your favorable consideration of Mr. Smith."* Then close the door behind the voter.

➢ Be sure to drive slowly and carefully to the polls obeying all traffic laws along the way. When you arrive to the poll, open the vehicle door for the voter and again say, *"Please don't forget to consider voting for John Smith."* When the voter returns from the polling place be sure to open the door and help him/her in the vehicle. There is no reason not to be polite just because the voter has already cast his/her vote. Remember, the driver's actions will reflect on the candidate and may be the only contact the voter will have with the campaign.

Chapter 14
Getting the Results

At the end of the day, the polls are about to close, the phone calls have stopped and there is nothing more that can be done to influence the outcome of the election. But your work and that of certain volunteers is not finished just yet!

❖ A volunteer needs to be assigned at each polling place to take the results. It is always easiest to have the bingo checker that worked the last shift remain in the poll after it closes to record the results.

❖ That volunteer should be provided with a tally sheet that lists the precinct name, the district number, and the names of each candidate competing for your position.

❖ Next to the name of each candidate should be several lines (one for each voting machine in the precinct) to record the number of votes each candidate received.

❖ The poll warden will "open" the voting machine and yell out the name of each candidate on the ballot and the number of votes each candidate received.

❖ The volunteer needs to record the results carefully so that no mistakes are made. In the excitement of the moment, it is very easy to transpose numbers turning a tally of 123 votes into a tally of 213 votes. That could really cause havoc at headquarters.

❖ When the warden has finished reading all the results, verify the result with him one more time, then call the result into the volunteer coordinator at the headquarters.

❖ As the results from each polling place are called in to headquarters the campaign coordinator will verify the result twice before passing the numbers along to the volunteer for recording on the board for everyone to see.

Chapter 15
Reacting to the Election Results

The suspense in the room will mount until the final numbers are recorded, at which time the candidate will be expected to address the crowd of supporters. Naturally if your campaign was successful everyone will be happy and your remarks will come easy. If, on the other hand, the result was not favorable, you may need to take a little time before addressing the crowd assembled. Either way, make it a point to thank the volunteers for their extraordinary efforts and congratulate the opponent for a hard-fought campaign. Recognize any dignitaries that might be in the room and thank them as well. Win or lose, your next campaign may well be starting at this very moment so don't say anything that you don't want to see in the paper the next day or in an opponent's brochure in two or four years.

The remarks should be carefully planned and thought out as there is a good chance they will be recorded by the press. Immediately prior to delivering the remarks to supporters, a phone call to the opponent(s) would be in order. It is customary for the losing candidates to call and congratulate the winner. I always believed that the winner should initiate the calls since you will probably want to start mending fences right away and enlist this election's opponents as the next election's supporters.

Your remarks to your supporters should include a recap of the things you hope to accomplish over your term of office and a reminder of how grateful you are to them for helping you achieve your goals. Following your remarks, immediately fax or email a copy of your speech to any press outlets in your area that were not at the headquarters. Then take a few hours off. You'll need them.

Section IV
Ethical Public Service

Chapter 16
Honorable Service with Results

I will never forget a 1994 encounter I had with a friend of mine just a week or two after I was elected to my local town council for the very first time. He was a long-time member of the town council in a neighboring town and had risen to the level of council president. He was widely considered the heir-apparent to the long-reigning mayor and his political star had certainly been on the rise. One day he was taken down in an FBI sting operation that changed both his life and the political landscape of that town.

My wife and I bumped into him as we entered my favorite restaurant. He and his wife had just finished dinner and were on their way out. We spoke for a while about the impending federal prison term that he was about to begin and he offered advice that continues to ring in my ears to this very day. "Whatever you do," he said, "Don't get caught up in the glamour of the position. Don't believe anyone when they tell you that 'this is the way business is done here.' Always question what they are asking you to do and don't do anything you are uncomfortable with just because you don't want to make political waves."

I kept his advice foremost in my mind throughout the almost seventeen years I served on the town council. I was always on my proverbial toes and never took part in votes or activities simply as a means of securing my political future or solely to ingratiate myself with the powers that be.

In fact, on the contrary, I questioned authority. I parted ways with my council colleagues when I didn't agree with their position on the issues. Often I was the single "no" vote on an issue that passed 6 to 1 and just as frequently, I was the sole "yes" vote on issues that failed on the same 6-1 vote. Throughout my tenure, I remained keenly aware of the actions of my colleagues and learned to identify patterns in their voting, patterns that led me to question their motives and their integrity.

While many may have ignored those signs, I paid particular attention to them and was able to identify tell-tale signs that some were "selling their votes" to the highest bidders. I alerted the FBI and wore a wire for almost two years exposing one of the most corrupt municipal administrations in America. The efforts, and two investigative reports that I and another honest councilman co-authored, resulted in the arrests and convictions of three sitting councilmen including the sitting council president, a former council president, a former town solicitor, an on-air radio personality, an unlicensed insurance broker, a strip club manager who acted as a middle-man in paying the bribes, a zoning board member, and the town's acting finance director.

All but one pled guilty and the one that maintained his innocence was found guilty at trial. Five federal prison terms ranged from 1 year and a day to 6 years. Others were given home confinement or confinement to a half-way house followed by multi-year probationary periods. Still others were forced to relinquish their positions and pay substantial fines which, in some cases, exceeded $100,000. At this writing, the case is still on-going and one prominent businessman and his company await trial for bribing public officials.

Despite appearances, my entire council tenure was not consumed with fighting and exposing corruption. I was able to enact policies that had a substantial positive impact on the town. I fought to improve services while voting to keep taxes low. I was responsible for the initiation of a curbside recycling program, bicycle police patrols in the villages and a comprehensive program to reduce speeding on the town's secondary roads. I drafted, introduced and passed proposals to enact historic district zoning and a home-based business ordinance. I passed local ordinances preventing the zoning of adult entertainment facilities in neighborhoods or places where children congregate and increasing penalties for tobacco vendors who partake in the illegal but lucrative sale of tobacco products to children. I was responsible for ordinances to preserve open space, prohibit the use of eminent domain for commercial gain, making sidewalks accessible to people with disabilities and creating a program that enabled the local cable television station to air council meetings on TV for the very first time in the town's history. I even used my town council position to effectuate programs at the state level that increased the state penalties for the illegal sales of tobacco products to children that included, for the first time in state history, a provision to revoke the tobacco sales license for habitual offenders. And, I drafted, lobbied and was able to get enacted two state health laws; one prohibiting health insurance companies from including a pre-existing condition clause in insurance policies written in my state and one requiring health insurance companies to provide expanded coverage for the equipment, supplies and education necessary for the home treatment of diabetes. These two laws had a positive impact on the lives of over 1 million people in my state and actually reduced long-term insurance costs for the health insurers.

Each year, in addition to the routine business that came before the council, I focused on the passage of at least one new, innovative program that would improve the quality of life for the people I served. I never worried about what my political enemies were doing but instead focused all my energies on positive programs that would help people.

I believe it was that focus and my sincere efforts to try to improve people's lives and make a positive difference in my community that led to my successful public service career. This is the advice that I would offer anyone thinking of entering the political arena. It is too easy in public life to get sidetracked from the issues. It is too tempting to act negatively to punish or even try to "destroy" political enemies and those who would support them. That behavior might even lead to political longevity, but it will ruin you. It will detract from the reason you sought office in the first place and it will eventually get you in trouble.

Resist that temptation and the temptations that partisan politics place before you on a daily basis. Focus on doing what is right and on helping people legally and productively whether the proposal is being advocated by members of your party or by members of the opposition party.

When you reach the point in your elective career when fielding late-night calls from constituents and listening to their problems and concerns for hours on end becomes a chore, it is time to step aside and let someone else take over. Don't become a self-serving public servant. Rather, stay focused on doing good things. The rest will fall into place.

Conclusion

Running for public office is a major, and in some cases, a life-altering decision. It takes a significant amount of time, time that you will not be able to spend with your family. You may be attacked by forces that don't want you to run and your life will be far less private while you are running and while you are serving than it once was. Don't take the decision lightly and don't make it in a vacuum. Do your homework and explore all the reasons why you should or shouldn't seek office. Once you make a commitment, give your campaign effort 100% every-day, from the moment you decide to run until the time you go to bed on election-night.

Stay positive and focused on the task at hand – getting elected. Don't get sidetracked with small issues, political or otherwise, that arise during the course of day-to-day campaigning. Rather, develop a plan and stick to it. A well thought out plan is always worth adhering to. If you have done adequate planning early on, everything will fall into place when it needs to and you will be celebrating a victory on election night. Much like the marathon runner, if you do the hard work during training (the campaign), you will find that the race itself (election day), will be so much easier.

Congratulations on your desire and willingness to serve. Now go out and be the very best candidate and public servant that you can be.

Appendix

The sample forms provided here are not for use as each state may have its own specific forms or completely different requirements. These are provided only as examples of the type of form that may exist in your political jurisdiction.

- ❖ **Sample State Voter Registration Form** (From the RI Secretary of State's Office) p.149
- ❖ **Sample Federal Voter Registration Application.** p.150
- ❖ **2016 Election Calendar** (From the RI Secretary of State's Office) p. 151
- ❖ **Sample Campaign Finance Forms** (From the RI State Board of Elections) p.172
  - ➢ Notice of Organization
  - ➢ Summary of Campaign Activity
  - ➢ Schedule of Contributions Received
  - ➢ Schedule of Expenditures
  - ➢ Affidavit for Annual Filing Exemption
  - ➢ Affidavit Dissolving Campaign Account
  - ➢ 2016 Reporting Schedule
  - ➢ 2016 General Election Reporting Schedule
- ❖ **Sample Declaration of Candidacy Form** (From the RI Secretary of State's Office) p.190.
- ❖ **Sample Endorsement by Party Committee Form** (From the RI Secretary of State's Office. p.191
- ❖ **Sample Bingo Sheet.** p.192

Sample State Voter Registration Form

RHODE ISLAND
VOTER REGISTRATION FORM

Please print clearly in ink. All information is required unless marked optional.

YOU MAY USE THIS FORM TO:
* Register to vote in Rhode Island.
* Change your name and/or address on your registration.
* Choose a political party or change parties.

TO REGISTER TO VOTE IN RI YOU MUST BE:
* A legal resident of Rhode Island.
* A citizen of the United States.
* At least 16 years of age.
  (You must be at least 18 years of age to vote on Election Day.)

INSTRUCTIONS

Box 2: REQUIRED. Rhode Island citizens who are at least 16 years of age may pre-register to vote using this form. If you fail to check either of these boxes, this form will be returned to you. If you checked NO to either of these statements, do not complete this form.

Box 3: If you are registering to vote for the first time in Rhode Island by mail or if someone else turns this form in for you, it is REQUIRED that you provide your driver's license number or state ID number issued by the RI Department of Motor Vehicles (DMV). If you do not have either, you must provide the last 4 digits of your Social Security Number. If you do not provide the above information or it cannot be verified, you will be required to provide identification to an election official before voting. Acceptable forms of identification are on the Board of Elections website at http://www.elections.ri.gov or contact your local Board of Canvassers (see reverse side of this form).

Box 5: A person may have only one legal residence. You must register from your legal residence. A post office box or rural route may only be used as a "Mailing Address" in Box 6.

Box 9: If you want to affiliate to vote, choose a party. If you leave Box 9 blank, you will be listed as unaffiliated.

Box 10: You must SIGN and DATE the registration form. If you fail to sign and date the form, it will be returned to you.

Box 11: If you are updating your voter registration because you legally changed your name, enter your previous legal name.

Box 12: If you are updating your voter registration because of an address change, enter your previous address, even if out-of-state.

You will receive an acknowledgement receipt of this voter registration form within 3 weeks. If you do not receive it, contact your local Board of Canvassers (see reverse side for list). For questions and deadlines relating to this form, visit the Board of Elections website at http://www.elections.ri.gov or contact your local Board of Canvassers (see reverse side for list).
(This form may be reproduced)

---

1. Check Boxes that Apply: ☐ New Voter Registration ☐ Address Change ☐ Party Change ☐ Name Change

2. I am a U.S. Citizen and resident of Rhode Island. ☐ Yes ☐ No

I am at least 16 years of age. (You must be at least 18 years of age to vote.) ☐ Yes ☐ No

If you checked NO to either of these statements, do not complete this form.

3. RI driver's license or ID Number: _____

If you do not have a RI driver's license or ID, enter last 4 digits of your social security number: _____

If you do not enter either number, see instructions for Box 3.

4. Last Name | Suffix (if any) | First Name | Middle Name (or initial)

5. Home Address (Do not enter a post office box) | Apt. | City/Town | State **RI** | ZIP Code

6. Mailing Address (If different from Box 5) | Apt. | City/Town | State | ZIP Code

7. Date of Birth (mm/dd/yyyy) — Month Day Year | **8.** Phone No./ E-mail Address (optional) | **9.** Party Affiliation ☐ Democrat ☐ Moderate ☐ Republican ☐ Unaffiliated ☐ Other _____

10. I swear or affirm that:
- I am not incarcerated in a correctional facility upon a felony conviction.
- I am not presently judged "mentally incompetent" to vote by a court of law.
- The information I have provided is true to the best of my knowledge under penalty of perjury. If I have provided false information, I may be fined, imprisoned, or (if not a U.S. citizen) deported from or refused entry into the United States.

Official Use For Barcode

PLEASE SIGN FULL NAME OR PLACE MARK BELOW

Date: (mm/dd/yyyy)
Signed

Are you interested in working at the polls? (check box below) ☐

Warning: If you sign this form and know it to be false, you can be convicted and fined up to $5,000 or jailed up to 10 years.

11. PREVIOUS NAME (if different from Box 4) | **12.** PREVIOUS ADDRESS OF REGISTRATION (City/Town, State, ZIP & County)

Sample Federal Voter Registration Form

Are you a citizen of the United States of America? ☐ Yes ☐ No Will you be 18 years old on or before election day? ☐ Yes ☐ No If you checked "No" in response to either of these questions, do not complete form. (Please see state-specific instructions for rules regarding eligibility to register prior to age 18.)	This space for office use only.

1 | ☐ Mr. ☐ Miss Last Name ☐ Mrs. ☐ Ms. | First Name | Middle Name(s) | ☐ Jr ☐ II
☐ Sr ☐ III ☐ IV

2 | Home Address | Apt. or Lot # | City/Town | State | Zip Code

3 | Address Where You Get Your Mail If Different From Above | City/Town | State | Zip Code

4 | Date of Birth ___ ___ ___ Month Day Year
5 | Telephone Number (optional)
6 | ID Number - (See item 6 in the instructions for your state)

7 | Choice of Party (see item 7 in the instructions for your State)
8 | Race or Ethnic Group (see item 8 in the instructions for your State)

9 | I have reviewed my state's instructions and I swear/affirm that:
- I am a United States citizen
- I meet the eligibility requirements of my state and subscribe to any oath required.
- The information I have provided is true to the best of my knowledge under penalty of perjury. If I have provided false information, I may be fined, imprisoned, or (if not a U.S. citizen) deported from or refused entry to the United States.

Please sign full name (or put mark) ▲

Date: ___ / ___ / ___
Month Day Year

If you are registering to vote for the first time: please refer to the application instructions for information on submitting copies of valid identification documents with this form.

Please fill out the sections below if they apply to you.

If this application is for a **change of name**, what was your name before you changed it?

A | ☐ Mr. ☐ Miss Last Name ☐ Mrs. ☐ Ms. | First Name | Middle Name(s) | ☐ Jr ☐ II
☐ Sr ☐ III ☐ IV

If you were **registered before** but this is the first time you are registering from the address in Box 2, what was your address where you were registered before?

B | Street (or route and box number) | Apt. or Lot # | City/Town/County | State | Zip Code

If you live in a rural area but do not have a street number, or if you have no address, please show on the map where you live.

C
- Write in the names of the crossroads (or streets) nearest to where you live.
- Draw an X to show where you live.
- Use a dot to show any schools, churches, stores, or other landmarks near where you live, and write the name of the landmark.

NORTH ↑

Example
Route #2
● Grocery Store
Woodchuck Road
Public School ●
X

If the applicant is unable to sign, who helped the applicant fill out this application? Give name, address and phone number (phone number optional).

D

Mail this application to the address provided for your State.

Paul F. Caranci

✓ VOTE
NOVEMBER 8

Nellie M. Gorbea
Secretary of State

Bring an ID to the polls

Poll workers will ask you to show a Photo ID when you vote at your polling place. Voter ID strengthens the public's faith in the integrity of our elections by enabling poll workers to match a voter's name to their face.

What is an acceptable Photo ID?

IDs must be valid and cannot have expired, but they do not need to have your current address.

Acceptable Photo IDs include:

› RI driver's license
› U.S. passport
› State of RI or U.S. government-issued ID card
› ID card from an educational institution in the United States
› U.S. military ID card
› Government-issued medical card
› Voter ID

Protecting Your Vote

No eligible voter will be turned away at the polls. Voters who do not bring ID to the polls can vote using a standard provisional ballot, which will be counted if the signature they give at the polling place matches the signature on their voter registration card.

Mail ballots will not require Voter ID.

If you don't have a valid photo ID? Get a free Voter ID.

Find out what documents you need to get a voter ID at www.sos.ri.gov

Contact us:

 elections@sos.ri.gov 401.222.2340   sos.ri.gov

Dear Local Elections Official:

As your Secretary of State, I am working hard to engage and empower all Rhode Islanders and ensure that our elections are fair, fast, and accurate. This digital guide contains all of the information and key dates you will need to administer the September primary and November's general election.

Some of the information included in this guide:

• Filing dates for candidate

•   oter registration deadlines

• Contact info for fellow elections official

We also encourage you to print out the flyers on the final pages of this guide to post in your offices for local voters. While this guide is offered electronically to make it easier for you to share it with your colleagues, we are happy to provide a hard copy of the guide or the Voter ID flyer upon request. If you need additional information, please contact our Elections Division at 401-222-2340, TTY 711 or elections@sos.ri.gov.

Government can and must be effective, transparent and accountable to the people it serves in order to succeed. That can only happen when we all participate. As a local elections official, I know that you work hard to make sure that Rhode Islanders who are eligible to vote, participate in our democratic process. I thank you for also working to make sure that our elections run smoothly.

Sincerely,

Nellie M. Gorbea *Secretary*
of State

Table of Contents

Notes:

> Rhode Island General Laws, [RIGL §17-1-7], provides for a uniform deadline of 4 p.m. unless another time is specified.

> The determinations herein are a matter of interpretation and are intended solely as a guide. They do not constitute official interpretation of state law.

> All statutory references are to Title 17 of the Rhode Island General Laws, 1956, as amended as of December 31, 2015.

> The Department of State will post changes to Title 17 that affect this election calendar on our website at www.sos.ri.gov. There will be a link on the Elections Division page that will take you to the status of any laws affecting the dates in this guide.

ELECTION CALENDAR HIGHLIGHTS

› **March 25, 26 and 27**
Disaffiliation for candidates

› **May 23, 24 and 25**
Deadline to register to vote in order to file a declaration of candidacy. (If filing declaration on June 23rd you must be registered by May 23rd. If filing declaration on June 24th you must be registered by May 24th. If filing declaration on June 25th you must be registered by May 25th.)

› **June 11**
Last day for disaffiliation for primary voters

› **June 23, 24 and 25**
Declaration of candidacy filing period. (All candidates for federal and statewide office file with the Secretary of State's Elections Division; all candidates for general assembly, local offices, Democratic state committee, district committees and local committees file with local boards of canvassers where the candidate is a registered voter.)

› **August 10**
Deadline to register to vote in the party primaries

› **September 9**
PRIMARIES

› **October 5**
Deadline to register to vote in the general election

› **November 4**
GENERAL ELECTION

Election Calendar Highlights

Disaffiliation for candidates

Deadline to register to file Declaration of Candidacy
Deadline for candidates to register to vote in order to be eligible to file a Declaration of Candidacy.

Last day for disaffiliation for primary voters

Declaration of Candidacy filing period
Declaration of Candidacy filing period. (All candidates for federal office and independent presidential electors file with the Department of State's Elections Division; all candidates for general assembly, local offices, district committees and local committees file with local boards of canvassers where the candidate is a registered voter.)

Deadline to register to vote in the party primaries

PARTY PRIMARIES

Deadline to register to vote in the general election

GENERAL ELECTION

2016 Election
Calendar and Explanations

March 29, 30 and 31

Disaffiliation - candidates
Deadline to file disaffiliation to run as a candidate. If you wish to run as a candidate and are affiliated with a political party other than the party in which you wish to run, you must disaffiliate at your local board of canvassers by this time. Deadline depends on date you file your Declaration of Candidacy.
[RIGL §17-14-1.1]

May 27

Registration - candidates
Deadline for candidates to register to vote in order to be eligible to file a Declaration of Candidacy. Persons must be registered to vote at least 30 days before filing their Declaration of Candidacy. [RIGL §17-14-1.2(a)]

June 15

Disaffiliation - primary voters
Deadline for voters to disaffiliate (if necessary) at their local board of canvassers in order to vote in a different party's primary. If you wish to disaffiliate you must do so at least 90 days prior to the primary. Unaffiliated voters may vote in any party's primary. [RIGL §17-9.1-24(a)]

June 27, 28 and 29

Declarations of Candidacy
Dates for filing declarations to be candidates in primaries or to be independent candidates in the general election. Candidates for federal office and independent presidential electors file with the Department of State's Elections Division. Candidates for general assembly, local offices, district committees and local committees file with local boards of canvassers where the candidate is registered to vote. [RIGL §17-14-1]

June 30

Party nominations
For any state office for which no primary nomination has been made and any local office for which no nomination has been made by any authorized city, town, ward, or district committee or any duly authorized subcommittee, state committees of political parties may file party nominations within 24 hours of the deadline for the filing of declarations of candidacy in the same location where the individual nominated would have filed their declaration of candidacy for such office. [RIGL §17-12-2(3)]

June 30

District endorsements
District committees file with local boards of canvassers lists of candidates having district committee endorsement (senatorial and representative district committees from the City of Providence file with the Department of State's Elections Division). To be filed not later than the day after the final day for filing declarations of candidacy. [RIGL §17-12-11(b)(2)(c)]

June 30   **City/Town/Ward endorsements**
City, town and ward committees file with local boards of canvassers lists of local candidates having committee endorsements. To be filed not later than the day after the final day for filing declarations of candidacy. [RIGL §17-12-11(a)(1)]

July 1   **State committee endorsements**
State committee notifies the Department of State's Elections Division of the endorsement of candidates to be voted upon by congressional district. To be filed not later than the second day after the final day for filing declarations of candidacy.

State committee to file with local boards of canvassers lists of candidates having committee endorsement when city, town or district committees have failed or neglected to do so. To be filed within 24 hours after city, town or district committees have failed to endorse. [RIGL §17-12-4]

July 6   **Nomination papers**
First day nomination papers are available. Candidates for federal office and independent presidential electors (or their designees) obtain nomination papers from the Department of State's Elections Division. Candidates (or their designees) for the following offices from the City of Providence obtain their nomination papers from the Department of State's Elections Division: senator, representative, and senatorial and representative district committees. All other general assembly, local office, district committee and local committee candidates obtain nomination papers from local boards of canvassers where they filed their declaration. Local board prepares within 2 business days of the final day of filing endorsements. (July 1st is final day for endorsement; July 2nd is a Saturday; July 3rd is a Sunday; July 4th is a holiday; July 5th is first business day; July 6th is second business day.) [RIGL §17-1-7]

Persons other than candidates picking up nomination papers from the Department of State's Elections Division (148 West River Street, Providence, RI) must have written authorization from the candidate. [RIGL §17-14-4(a)(c)]

July 15   **Nomination papers - COMPLETED**
All candidates (or their designees) except electors for independent presidential candidates, file completed nomination papers with local boards of canvassers. To be filed on or before the 60th day before the primary. [RIGL §17-14-11]

July 18   **Objections to candidates for local offices**
Final date to file objections to eligibility of candidates or sufficiency of nomination papers for local offices. Objections to be filed with the local board of canvassers the next business day after the final date for filing nomination papers. (July 16th is a Saturday; July 17th is a Sunday; July 18th is the first business day.) [RIGL §17-14-13]

July 18   **Withdrawals of candidates from local offices**
Final date for local candidates to file withdrawals of candidacy. To be filed where nomination papers were filed. Note: in the event an objection has been filed, withdrawal to be filed within 24 hours of decision. [RIGL §17-14-15]

157

July 20

Decisions on objections to candidates for local offices
Local boards of canvassers to make decisions on objections to eligibility of candidates or sufficiency of nomination papers for candidates for local offices. Decisions to be made within 2 days of objections, exclusive of Sundays and holidays. [RIGL §17-14-14(b)(c)]

July 21

Nomination papers - certification
Last day for local boards of canvassers to file primary and independent nomination papers for federal and state offices, and certifications for local offices with the Department of State's Elections Division. Local boards to file not later than 54 days prior to the primary. [RIGL §17-14-12]

July 22

Objections to candidates for federal and state offices
Final date to file objections to eligibility of candidates or sufficiency of nomination papers for all federal and state offices. Objections to be filed with the Department of State's Elections Division by the next business day after the final date for filing nomination papers. [RIGL §17-14-13]

July 22

Withdrawals of candidates from federal and state offices
Final date for federal and state candidates to file withdrawals of candidacy. To be filed where nomination papers were filed. Note: in the event an objection has been filed, withdrawal to be filed within 24 hours of decision. [RIGL §17-14-15]

July 22 at 5 p.m.

Lottery for primary ballot
The Department of State will conduct a lottery to determine ballot placement for unendorsed federal and state party candidates on primary ballots. The lottery will be held at 5 p.m. in the Governor's State Room, State House. If decision rendered on July 25th removes a candidate involved in the lottery, candidate's name will be removed from the ballot. [RIGL §17-15-8]

July 22 at 5 p.m.

Lottery for election ballot
The Department of State will conduct a lottery to determine ballot placement
of recognized political parties and independent candidates (except electors for independent presidential candidates - see September 16) for the general election ballots. The lottery will be held at 5 p.m. in the Governor's State Room, State House. [RIGL §17-19-9.1]

July 25

Decisions on objections to candidates for federal and state offices Board of Elections to make decisions on objections to eligibility of candidates or sufficiency of nomination papers for candidates for federal and state offices. Decisions to be made within 2 days of objections, exclusive of Sundays and holidays. [RIGL §17-14-14(a)(b)]

August 1

Submit list of officials - primaries
City/Town committees submit names to local board of canvassers of registered voters who will serve as wardens, moderators, supervisors and clerks.
[RIGL §§17-11-11, 17-15-13]

August 1	**Braille/tactile mail ballot requests** Final date for those voters who are blind or visually impaired to request a Braille or a tactile primary mail ballot from their local board of canvassers. [RIGL §17-19-8.1(b)]
August 9	**Appointment of officials - primaries** Local boards of canvassers to appoint wardens, moderators, supervisors and clerks at least 35 days prior to the primaries. [RIGL §17-15-13]
August 10	**Local questions** Local boards of canvassers to certify to the Department of State's Elections Division a copy of each question to be submitted to the electors of the city or town. To be done not later than the 90th day before the election. [RIGL §17-19-7]
August 13	**Canvass notice** Local boards of canvassers to post and advertise notice of canvass at least 10 days prior to canvass. Notice to be posted not later than August 13th in order for canvass to be conducted by August 23rd. [RIGL §17-10-5(a)]
August 14	**Voter registration deadline - primaries** Final date for voter registration for primaries. Registration must be made at least 30 days prior to the primary. [RIGL §§17-1-3, 17-1-7]
August 19	**Voter lists - preliminary** Local boards of canvassers to prepare and post preliminary lists of voters eligible to vote in the primaries. To be posted forthwith after close of voter registration for the primary. In accordance with chapter 17-9.1, certain registrations processed on the last day to register to vote are allowed a 5-day transmittal period. Accordingly, local boards of canvassers cannot prepare and post preliminary lists of eligible voters until after this 5-day transmittal period. [RIGL §17-10-3(a)]
within 5 days of posting preliminary voting list	**Voter lists - names erroneously included or omitted** Affidavit to be filed with local boards of canvassers by person claiming that their name has been erroneously included or omitted from the preliminary voting lists. To be done within 5 days of posting of preliminary voting lists. [RIGL §17-13-2]
August 23	**Mail ballot applications** Final date to submit application for a regular mail ballot for primaries. To be received by local boards of canvassers not later than 21 days prior to primaries. [RIGL §17-20-2.1(c)]
August 23	**Voter lists** Local boards of canvassers are to canvass and correct voting lists before the 20th day prior to primaries (20th day is August 24th – must be done before this date). [RIGL §17-10-5(a)]

August 24

Emergency mail ballots
Beginning of the period for emergency mail ballot applications for those voters whose circumstances necessitating a mail ballot arise during the period from August 24th through September 12th at 4 p.m. [RIGL §17-20-2.2(a)(b)]

August 26

Voting lists - final - primaries
Local boards of canvassers to post final corrected copies of voting lists for primaries. [RIGL §§17-10-5(a), 17-10-14]

August 26

Mail ballots - certification
Final day for local boards of canvassers to certify mail ballot applications to
the Department of State's Elections Division not later than 18 days prior to the primaries, or within 7 days of receipt, whichever occurs first.
[RIGL §17-20-10(c)]

September 2

Posting notice - primaries
Local boards of canvassers to post notice of primaries in each voting district.
To be done at least 8 days prior to primaries. Local boards of canvassers may substitute posting of notices by publication in the newspaper (September 5th is Labor Day). [RIGL §17-15-17]

September 6

Party officials - primaries
Local boards of canvassers to appoint watchers, checkers and runners for primaries. Appointments to be made from lists provided by city and town party committees at least 10 days prior to the primaries (September 3rd is a Saturday and September 5th is Labor Day). [RIGL §17-15-13(c)]

September 9

Nomination papers – completed – presidential electors for independent presidential candidates
All presidential electors for independent presidential candidates submit nomination papers to local boards of canvassers. To be filed on or before the 60th day before election. [RIGL §17-14-11]

September 12 at 4 p.m.

Emergency ballot applications
Final date to submit application for emergency ballot for primaries. To be received by local boards of canvassers not later than 4 p.m. [RIGL §17-20-2.2(b)]

September 13

Party Primaries
[RIGL §17-15-1]

September 13 at 8 p.m.

Mail ballots
Final date for receipt of mail ballots by Board of Elections for primaries. Must be received by the Board of Elections at 50 Branch Avenue, Providence, RI not later than 8 p.m. [RIGL §17-20-16]

160

September 14

Tabulation of returns
Local boards of canvassers to meet and tabulate city and town primary returns as the case may be, and announce results. Certificates of nomination or election not to be issued until expiration of period for requesting recount, and if recount is requested, following decision thereon. [RIGL §17-15-30(a)]

September 14

Recount requests
Final date for candidates to request Board of Elections to conduct a recount of votes cast at a specific voting location or locations, or for filing other protests concerning the primary. Must be filed not later than the day following the primaries. [RIGL §17-15-34]

September 15

Nomination papers – certification – presidential electors for independent presidential candidates
Local boards of canvassers to file nomination papers for presidential electors for independent presidential candidates with the Department of State's Elections Division. Local boards shall certify nomination papers to the Department of State's Elections Division not later than 54 days before the date of the election. [RIGL §17-14-12]

September 15

Names of party and independent presidential candidates
The secretary or duly authorized individual of each national party shall certify to the Department of State's Elections Division the names of individuals nominated as the party's candidates for president and vice president. The names of independent candidates for president and vice president must also be submitted by the authorized individual for those political organizations that have qualified independent presidential electors. By regulation adopted May 15th, 1996 to be filed not later than 54 days before the date of the election.

September 16

Nomination papers – objections – presidential electors for independent presidential candidates
Final date to file objections to nomination papers for presidential electors for independent presidential candidates. Objections must be filed by the next business day after the final date for filing nomination papers. [RIGL §17-14-13]

September 16

Nomination withdrawals – presidential electors for independent presidential candidates
Presidential electors for independent presidential candidates file withdrawals with the Department of State's Elections Division. If an objection has been filed, withdrawals may be filed within 24 hours after the Board of Elections renders its decision. [RIGL §17-14-15]

September 16 at 5 p.m.

Lottery for presidential electors for independent presidential candidates
The Department of State will conduct a lottery to determine ballot placement
of presidential electors for independent presidential candidates for the general election ballots. Lottery will be held at 5 p.m. in the State Library, State House. (If decision rendered on September 19th removes presidential electors for a particular presidential candidate, the names will be removed from the ballot.)
[RIGL §17-19-9.1]

September 16 **Filling vacancies**
Final date for filling vacancies caused whenever a nominee of a recognized political party removes themselves from the jurisdiction of the district or as a candidate for the office for which the nominee seeks election. In the event of death, the vacancy can be filled at anytime. Vacancies must be filed in the same location where the individual would have filed their declaration of candidacy for such office. [RIGL §17-15-38(a)]

September 16 **Local candidates**
Local boards of canvassers to certify to the Department of State's Elections Division the names of candidates for each local office and the party name under which they were nominated, and the names of all qualified independent candidates for each local office. To be done not later than the third day following the date of the primaries. [RIGL §17-19-7]

September 19 **Nomination papers – decisions – presidential electors for independent presidential candidates**
Board of Elections to make decisions on objections to nomination papers for presidential electors for independent presidential candidates. Decision to be made within 2 days of objection, exclusive of Sundays and holidays.
[RIGL §17-14-14]

September 26 **Submit list of officials - general election**
City/Town committees submit names to local board of canvassers of registered voters who will serve as wardens, moderators, supervisors and clerks.
[RIGL §§17-11-11, 17-11-13]

September 26 **Braille/tactile mail ballot requests**
Final date for those voters who are blind or visually impaired to request a braille or a tactile general election mail ballot from their local board of canvassers.
[RIGL §17-19-8.1(b)]

October 4 **Appointment of officials - general election**
Local boards of canvassers to appoint officials for general election. Appointments to be made from lists provided by city and town committees at least 35 days prior to the general election. [RIGL §§17-11-11, 17-11-13(a)]

October 8 **Canvass notice**
Local boards of canvassers to post and advertise notice of canvass at least 10 days prior to canvass. Notice to be posted not later than October 8th in order for canvass to be conducted by October 18th. [RIGL §17-10-5(a)]

October 9 **Voter registration – general election**
Final date for voter registration for the general election. Registration must be made at least 30 days prior to the general election.
[RIGL §§§17-1-3, 17-1-7, 17-9.1-3]

October 14   **Voter list – preliminary**
Local boards of canvassers must prepare and post preliminary lists of voters eligible to vote in the general election. To be posted forthwith after close of voter registration for the general election.

In accordance with Chapter 17-9.1, certain registrations processed on the last day to register to vote are allowed a 5-day transmittal period. Accordingly, local boards of canvassers cannot prepare and post preliminary lists of eligible voters until after this 5-day transmittal period. [RIGL §17-10-3(a)]

Within 5 days of posting
of preliminary voting list   **Voter lists – names erroneously included or omitted**

Affidavit to be filed with local boards of canvassers by person claiming that their name has been erroneously included or omitted from the preliminary voting lists. To be done within 5 days of posting of preliminary voting lists. [RIGL §§17-10-5, 17-13-2]

October 14   **Party conventions**
State conventions for political parties in Rhode Island shall be held not later than October 14th. [RIGL §17-12-13]

October 18   **Mail ballot applications**
Final date to submit application for a regular mail ballot for the general election. To be received by local boards of canvassers not later than 21 days prior to the general election.

Exception: deadline to apply for a mail ballot to vote only for president and vice president is November 1st (Federal Voting Rights Act 1973aa-1(d)). [RIGL §17-20-2.1(c)]

October 18   **Voter lists**
Local boards of canvassers are to canvass and correct voting lists before the 20th day prior to the general election (20th day is October 19th – must be done before this date). [RIGL §17-10-5(a)]

October 19   **Emergency mail ballots**
Beginning of the period for emergency mail ballot applications for those voters whose circumstances necessitating a mail ballot arise during the period from October 19th through November 7th at 4 p.m. [RIGL §17-20-2.2(a)(b)]

October 21   **Voting lists – final – general election**
Local boards of canvassers to post final corrected copies of voting lists for the general election. [RIGL §17-10-14]

October 21   **Mail ballots – certification**
Final day for local boards of canvassers to certify mail ballot applications to the Department of State's Elections Division (not later than 18 days prior to the general election, or within 7 days of receipt, whichever occurs first). [RIGL §17-20-10(c)]

November 1	**Warrants – posting** Final day for city and town clerks to issue and post warrants notifying of the general election. To be issued and posted at least 7 days prior to Election Day.[RIGL §17-18-3]
November 7 at 4 p.m.	**Emergency ballot applications** Final date to submit application for emergency ballot for the general election. To be received by local boards of canvassers not later than 4 p.m. [RIGL §17-20-2.2(b)]
November 8	**Election Day** [RIGL §17-18-5]
November 8 at 8 p.m.	**Mail ballots** Final date for receipt of mail ballots by Board of Elections for the general election. Must be received by Board of Elections at 50 Branch Avenue, Providence, RI, not later than 8 p.m. [RIGL §17-20-16]
November 15	**Recount requests** Final date for candidates to request Board of Elections to conduct a recount of votes. Petition to be filed within 7 days after the election. [RIGL §§§17-1-7, 17-19-36, 17-19-37]
December 19	**Presidential electors** Meeting of presidential electors to be held at the State House at noon. [RIGL §17-4-11]
January, 2017	**Committees – organization** City, town and district committees to organize. [RIGL §17-12-9(a)]
Within 10 days of organization	**Committees – filings** City, town and district committees, within 10 days of organization, file lists of officers and members with the Department of State's Elections Division and local boards of canvassers. [RIGL §17-12-9(c)]

2016 Campaign Finance Calendar

Note: "NOTICE OF ORGANIZATION"

Any candidate for public office, as defined in §17-25-3, is required to file a "Notice of Organization" with the Board of Elections prior to receiving any contributions or expending any money in the furtherance or aid of his/her candidacy or at the time of filing his/her declaration of candidacy, whichever occurs first. (Note: Persons who have a "Notice" on file with the Board of Elections and who regularly file reports with the Board are required to file an amended "Notice" whenever there is a change to information therein contained.)

For further information regarding campaign finance requirements, contact:

Rhode Island State Board of Elections
50 Branch Avenue
Providence, Rhode Island 02904
Phone: 401-222-2345 - Fax: 401-222-4424
Email: campaign.finance@elections.ri.gov - Website: www.elections.ri.gov

February 1 (not later than) POLITICAL PARTY COMMITTEES – TREASURER

Designation of a campaign treasurer by each state and municipal committee of a political party. [§17-25-9]

March 1 **ANNUAL REPORTS**
Each state and municipal committee of a political party must file an annual report setting forth in the aggregate all contributions received and expenditures made during the previous calendar year. [§17-25-7(b)]

(For reporting period January 1, 2016 thru March 31, 2016)
May 2 **QUARTERLY ONGOING REPORTS**
Reports are due from candidates, political parties, and political action committees. [§17-25-11]

(For reporting period April 1, 2016 thru June 30, 2016) QUARTERLY
August 1 **ONGOING REPORTS**
Reports are due from candidates*, political parties, and political action committees.

* Candidates who file their "Notice of Organization" during the declaratio period need not file this report. The first report of contributions received and expenditures incurred shall be due as follows:

› IF A CANDIDATE IN THE PRIMARY, the report for the period between the date of declaration and August 15, 2016, shall be due on August 16, 2016.

› IF NO A CANDIDATE IN THE PRIMARY, the report for the period between the date of declaration and October 10, 2016, shall be due on October 11, 2016.

[§17-25-11]

(For reporting period July 1, 2016 thru August 15, 2016)
August 16 **PRE-PRIMARY REPORTS**
Candidates, political parties, and political action committees that are participating in a primary must file reports 28 days prior to the party primaries. [§17-25-11(a)(2)]

September 6

(For reporting period August 16, 2016 thru September 5, 2016)
PRE-PRIMARY REPORTS
Candidates, political parties, and political action committees that are participating in a primary must file reports 7 days prior to the party primaries. [§17-25-11(a)(2)]

October 11

PRE-ELECTION REPORTS
Candidates, political parties, and political action committees that are participating in the election must file reports 28 days prior to the election.

If the candidate, political party or political action committee:

› ARTICIPATED IN THE PRIMARY (Does not include unsuccessful primary candidates - See October 11, 2016) the reporting period is September 6, 2016 thru October 10, 2016.

› DID NO PARTICIPATE IN THE PRIMARY the reporting period is July 1, 2016 thru October 10, 2016. [§17-25-11(a)(2)]

October 11

(For reporting period September 6, 2016 thru October 10, 2016)
POST-PRIMARY REPORTS – UNSUCCESSFUL PRIMARY CANDIDATES All unsuccessful primary candidates must file reports 28 days after the primary. [§17-25-11(a)(3)]

October 31

(For reporting period July 1, 2016 thru September 30, 2016)
QUARTERLY ONGOING REPORTS
Reports are due from candidates, political parties and political action committees that are not participating in the September primary or November election.
[§17-25-11]

November 1

(For reporting period October 11, 2016 thru October 31, 2016)
PRE-ELECTION REPORTS
Candidates, political parties, and political action committees that are participating in the election must file reports 7 days prior to the election. [§17-25-11(a)(2)]

December 6

(For reporting period November 1, 2016 thru December 5, 2016)
POST-ELECTION REPORTS
Candidates, political parties, and political action committees that participated in the election must file reports 28 days after the election. [§17-25-11(a)(3)]

QUARTERLY ONGOING REPORTS
Reports are due from all candidates, political parties, and political action committees.

If the candidate, political party or political action committee:

January 31, 2017

› ARTICIPATED IN THE NOVEMBER 8, 2016 ELECTION the reporting period is December 6, 2016 thru December 31, 2016.

› AS UNSUCCESSFUL IN THE PRIMARY the reporting period is October 11, 2016 thru December 31, 2016.

› DID NO PARTICIPATE IN A PRIMARY OR ELECTION the reporting period is October 1, 2016 thru December 31, 2016. [§17-25-11]

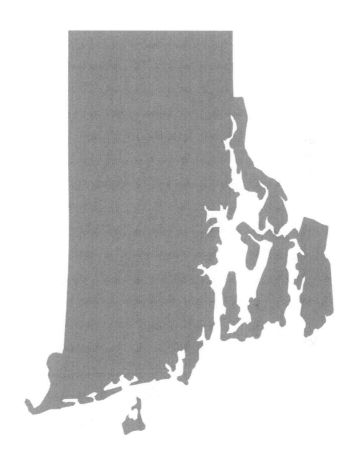

Qualifications for Elective Office

Office	Age	State Residence	U.S. Citizen Term	Years in	# of Terms
President	35	14 years in U.S.	yes, natural born	4	2
Vice President	35	14 years in U.S.	yes, natural born	4	no limit
Presidential Elector	18	30 days	yes	n/a	no limit
U.S. Senator *	30	yes	9 years	6	no limit
U.S. Representative	25	yes	7 years	2	no limit
State Senator	18	30 days	yes	2	no limit
State Representative	18	30 days	yes	2	no limit

*Not on the ballot in 2016

Polling Place Hours Opening Times of Polls

CITY/TOWN	OPEN A.M.	CITY/TOWN	OPEN A.M.
Barrington	7 a.m.	Newport	7 a.m.
Bristol	7 a.m.	New Shoreham	9 a.m.
Burrillville	7 a.m.*	North Kingstown	7 a.m.
Central Falls	7 a.m.	North Providence	7 a.m.
Charlestown	7 a.m.*	North Smithfield	7 a.m.
Coventry	7 a.m.	Pawtucket	7 a.m.
Cranston	7 a.m.	Portsmouth	7 a.m.
Cumberland	7 a.m.	Providence	7 a.m.
East Greenwich	7 a.m.	Richmond	7 a.m.
East Providence	7 a.m.	Scituate	7 a.m.
Exeter	7 a.m.	Smithfield	7 a.m.
Foster	7 a.m.	South Kingstown	7 a.m.
Glocester	7 a.m.	Tiverton	7 a.m.
Hopkinton	7 a.m.*	Warren	7 a.m.
Jamestown	7 a.m.**	Warwick	7 a.m.
Johnston	7 a.m.	Westerly	7 a.m.*
Lincoln	7 a.m.	West Greenwich	7 a.m.
Little Compton	7 a.m.*	West Warwick	7 a.m.
Middletown	7 a.m.	Woonsocket	7 a.m.
Narragansett	7 a.m.		

* in primary elections in the towns of Burrillville, Charlestown, Hopkinton, Little Compton and esterly polls shall open at 9 a.m.

** in primary elections in the town of Jamestown polls shall open at 8 a.m

Closing Times of Polls

The polls in all cities and towns in Rhode Island will remain open for voting until 8 p.m.

Any person eligible to vote who is in line to vote at 8 p.m. will be allowed to cast his or her vote before the polls close.

169

Local Boards of Canvassers
Contact Information

Hopkinton Town Hall
1 Town House Rd. 02833
377-7777

Jamestown Town Hall
93 Narragansett Ave. 02835
423-9804

Johnston Town Hall
1385 Hartford Ave. 02919
553-8856

Lincoln Town Hall
100 Old River Rd.
P.O. Box 100 02865
333-1140

Little Compton Town Hall
40 Commons
P.O. Box 226 02837
635-4400

Middletown Town Hall
350 East Main Rd. 02842
849-5540

Narragansett Town Hall
25 Fifth Ave. 02882
782-0625

Newport City Hall
43 Broadway 02840
845-5386

New Shoreham Town Hall
16 Old Town Rd.
P.O. Box 220 02807
466-3200

North Kingstown Town Hall
80 Boston Neck Rd. 02852
294-3331 x128

North Providence Town Hall
2000 Smith St. 02911
232-0900 x234

North Smithfield Municipal Annex
575 Smithfield Rd. 02896
767-2200

Pawtucket City Hall
137 Roosevelt Ave. 02860
722-1637

Portsmouth Town Hall
2200 East Main Rd. 02871
683-3157

Providence City Hall
25 Dorrance St. 02903
421-0495

Richmond Town Hall
5 Richmond Townhouse
Rd. Wyoming 02898
539-9000 x9

Scituate Town Hall
195 Danielson Pike
P.O. Box 328, N. Scituate
02857 647-7466

Smithfield Town Hall
64 Farnum Pike
Esmond 02917
233-1000 x112

South Kingstown Town Hall 180 High St.
Wakefield 02879
789-9331 x1231

Tiverton Town Hall
343 Highland Rd. 02878
625-6703

Warren Town Hall
514 Main St. 02885
245-7340 x4

Warwick City Hall
3275 Post Rd. 02886
738-2000

West Greenwich Town Hall 280 Victory Hwy.
02817
392-3800

West Warwick Town Hall
1170 Main St. 02893
822-9201

Westerly Town Hall
45 Broad St. 02891
348-2503

Woonsocket City Hall
169 Main St.
P.O. Box B 02895
767-9223

Portsmouth Town Hall
2200 East Main Rd. 02871
683-3157

Providence City Hall
25 Dorrance St. 02903
421-0495

Richmond Town Hall
5 Richmond Townhouse
Rd. Wyoming 02898
539-9000 x9

Scituate Town Hall
195 Danielson Pike
P.O. Box 328, N. Scituate
02857 647-7466

Smithfield Town Hall
64 Farnum Pike
Esmond 02917
233-1000 x112

South Kingstown Town Hall 180 High St.
Wakefield 02879
789-9331 x1231

Tiverton Town Hall
343 Highland Rd. 02878
625-6703

Warren Town Hall
514 Main St. 02885
245-7340 x4

Warwick City Hall
3275 Post Rd. 02886
738-2000

West Greenwich Town Hall 280 Victory Hwy.
02817
392-3800

West Warwick Town Hall
1170 Main St. 02893
822-9201

Westerly Town Hall
45 Broad St. 02891
348-2503

Woonsocket City Hall
169 Main St.
P.O. Box B 02895
767-9223

State Elections and Political Party Offices
Contact Information

> **Department of State**
> Elections Division   222-2340
> 148 W. River St., Providence, RI 02904

> **Board of Elections**   222-2345
> 50 Branch Ave., Providence, RI 02904

> **Rhode Island Democratic Party**   272-3367
> 200 Metro Center Blvd., Suite 1, Warwick, RI 02886

> **Moderate Party of Rhode Island**   932-8364
> 209 Yorktown Rd., North Kingstown, RI 02852

> **Rhode Island Republican Party**   732-8282
> 1800 Post Rd., Suite 17-I, Warwick, RI 02886

Department of State's Website

The following information concerning the 2016 election cycle will be found at: www.sos.ri.gov/elections

> Election Calendar - English & Spanish
> How to Run for Office Guide - English & Spanish - Available soon
> How to Register and Vote Guide - English & Spanish - Available soon
> Declaration of Candidacy Form - Available soon
> Political Party Endorsement Form - Available soon
> Qualified Federal and State Candidates: Starting June 28, 2016, daily updates of federal and state candidates who filed and/or qualified for ballot placement
> Qualified Local Candidates: Starting June 28, 2016, daily updates of local candidates who filed and/or qualified for ballot placement
> Sample ballots
> Find your polling place
> Mail Ballot Applications - Available soon
> Voter Referenda Handbook - Available September, 2016

Campaign Finance Forms

State of Rhode Island and Providence Plantations
Board of Elections
Campaign Finance Unit
50 Branch Avenue, Providence, Rhode Island 02904
Telephone No. (401) 222-2345
www.elections.ri.gov

SUMMARY OF BALLOT QUESTION ADVOCACY ACTIVITY (BQA-1)

Office Time Stamp

Full Name of Ballot Question Advocate

Other Name(s) Under Which Ballot Question Advocacy Conducted

Street Address	City/Town, State and Zip Code	
Mailing Address (if different)	City/Town, State and Zip Code	

Telephone Number	Daytime Telephone Number	Fax Number	E-mail Address

Name(s) and Address(es) of Endorsing or Member Organizations of This Ballot Question Advocate that have authorized the Ballot Question Advocate to use their name in support of their efforts: (Attach additional list if necessary)

Name	Address

The Question Whose Approval or Rejection the Ballot Question Advocate Intends to Advocate

Ballot Question: _____ ☐ Approval ☐ Rejection

Summary of Activity for Reporting Period (see reverse for instructions)

Reporting Period Beginning Date: _____ ☐ Original Report

Reporting Period Ending Date: _____ ☐ Amended Report

Beginning Fund Balance: $ _____

Plus: Total Amount Contributed This Period: $ _____

Minus: Total Amount Expended This Period: ($ _____)

Ending Fund Balance: $ _____

In-Kind Contributions This Period: $ _____

Pursuant to R.I.G.L. 17-25.2-5(a)(1): The Name, Address and, if applicable, the Place of Employment of every person making a contribution(s) that in the aggregate exceed $1,800 per election cycle to a ballot question advocate for the purpose of ballot question advocacy must be identified.

☐ See attached "Schedule of Contributions For Ballot Advocacy"

(Form BQA-2) for Identified Contributions.

Pursuant to R.I.G.L. 17-25.2-5(a)(2): The Name and Address of every person or entity receiving an expenditure for ballot question advocacy, which in the aggregate exceeds $100, must be identified.

☐ See attached "Schedule of Expenditures For Ballot Advocacy"

(Form BQA-3) for Identified Expenditures.

I hereby certify that this report of contributions and expenditures and the supporting documents are complete, true and correct and that I am responsible for its contents and for the ballot question advocate's compliance with the provisions of R.I.G.L. 17-25.2.

Print Name of Person Completing Report/Officer of the Ballot Question Advocate

Title of Person Completing Report/Officer of the Ballot Question Advocate

X _____
Signature of Person Completing Report or   Date
An Officer of the Ballot Question Advocate

Address of Person Completing Report/Officer of the Ballot Question Advocate

BQA-1   09/12

INSTRUCTIONS

Full Name of Ballot Question Advocate – Enter the full name of the Ballot Question Advocate (For purposes of statewide referenda only, any exempt nonprofit as defined in section 17-25-3 or any organization described under section 501(c)(3) of the Internal Revenue Code; and for all other ballot questions, any person making an expenditure with a cumulative total that exceeds one thousand dollars ($1,000) in a calendar year for ballot question advocacy on a particular ballot question.)

Other Name(s) Under Which Ballot Advocacy Conducted – Enter any other name under the ballot question advocate conducts ballot question advocacy.

Street Address – Enter the address of the ballot question advocate.

City/Town, State & Zip Code – Enter the City/Town, State and Zip Code of the ballot question advocate.

Mailing Address – Enter the address where mail is directed to this ballot question advocate, if different from the mailing address.

City/Town, State and Zip Code – Enter the City/Town, State and Zip Code where mail is directed to this ballot question advocate, if different from the mailing address.

Telephone Number – Enter the telephone number of the ballot question advocate.

Daytime Telephone Number – Enter a secondary telephone for the ballot question advocate.

Fax Number – Enter the fax number for this ballot question advocate.

E-mail Address – Enter the E-mail address for this ballot question advocate.

Names and Addresses of Endorsing or Member Organizations – Enter the names and addresses of all identified endorsing or member organizations, corporations, and/or associations that authorize the ballot question advocate to represent to the public that they support the ballot question advocate.

Question Whose Approval/Rejection the Ballot Question Advocate Intends to Advocate – Identify the ballot question for which the ballot question advocate intends to advocate and check the appropriate box to indicate whether the advocacy shall be the approval or rejection of said ballot question.

Original Report – Check this box if the report being filed is the initial report for this Reporting Period.

Amended Report – Check this box if the report being filed contains changes from the initial report for this Reporting Period.

Reporting Period Beginning Date – Enter the first date of the reporting period.

Reporting Period Ending Date – Enter the last date of the reporting period.

The first report must be filed for the period beginning when the ballot question advocate expends a cumulative total that exceeds one thousand dollars ($1,000) for the ballot question advocacy and ending the last day of the first full month following such date, to be filed with the Board of Elections due no late than seven (7) days after the end of the month. Reports must be filed thereafter for each calendar month due no later than seven (7) days after the end of each month; provided that in lieu of filing for the last full calendar month preceding the ballot question election, a report must be filed due no later than seven (7) days before the election. A final report must be filed no later than thirty (30) days after the election.

Beginning Fund Balance: – Enter the amount of total funds this Ballot Question Advocate has as of the first date of the reporting period. Note: This amount should be the same amount as the Ending Fund Balance reported on this advocate's last filed report.

Total Amount Contributed This Period – Enter the total amount contributed by each person or source, excluding in-kind contributions, to this ballot question advocate in this reporting period. Contributions, including in-kind, received in excess of one thousand eight hundred dollars ($1,800) in aggregate from any person per election cycle must also be disclosed on a "Schedule of Contributions For Ballot Advocacy" (Form BQA-2) and should be so noted by checking the appropriate box.

Total Amount Expended This Period – Enter the total amount expended by this ballot question advocate in this reporting period. Expenditures made in excess of one hundred dollars ($100) in aggregate to any person or entity must also be disclosed on a "Schedule of Expenditures For Ballot Advocacy" (Form BQA-3) and should be so noted by checking the appropriate box.

Ending Fund Balance – Enter the total of (Beginning Fund Balance + Total Contributions This Period) – Total Expenditures This Period.

In-Kind Contributions This Period – Enter the monetary value of other things of value or paid personal services donated to the Ballot Question Advocate, except for newsletters and other communications paid for and transmitted by the advocate to its own members and not to the general public.

Name/Title of Person Completing Report – The individual completing this report must affix his or her signature, thereby certifying this report of contributions and expenditures and the supporting documents is complete, true and accurate and who shall be responsible for its contents.

If you have any questions on how to complete this form, please contact the Board of Elections.

PENALTIES   Any person violating the provisions of the Rhode Island Ballot Advocacy and Reporting Act (Chapter 25.3 of Title 17 of the Rhode Island General Laws) shall be subject to penalties.

Please see reverse side for instructions on how to complete this form.

State of Rhode Island and Providence Plantations
Board of Elections
Campaign Finance Unit
50 Branch Avenue, Providence, Rhode Island 02904
Tel. (401) 222-2345
www.elections.ri.gov

SCHEDULE OF CONTRIBUTIONS FOR BALLOT ADVOCACY (BQA-2) | Office Time Stamp

Full Name of Ballot Question Advocate

Reporting Period Beginning Date: _____   ☐ Original Report

Reporting Period Ending Date: _____   ☐ Amended Report

NAME AND ADDRESS OF CONTRIBUTOR	PLACE OF EMPLOYMENT OF CONTRIBUTOR, IF INDIVIDUAL	DATE CONTRIBUTION RECEIVED	TRANSACTION TYPE (see back for list of types)	AMOUNT OF CONTRIBUTION

For Gambling Ballot Questions Only: List all contributors on this page who have a direct or indirect affiliation with any entity or person that operates or owns any type or kind of gambling facility or entity in any jurisdiction and, if so, the name of such facility or entity.

Contributor Name   Gambling Facility or Entity Name

_____   _____
_____   _____
_____   _____
_____   _____
_____   _____

PAGE NO: _____ OF _____   PAGE TOTAL (Do Not Include In-Kind) | $

BQA-2   07/06

INSTRUCTIONS

The information reported is required under the Rhode Island Ballot Advocacy and Reporting Act.

Full Name of Ballot Question Advocate – Enter the full name of the Ballot Question Advocate (Any person making an expenditure with a cumulative total that exceeds one thousand dollars ($1,000) in a calendar year for ballot question advocacy on a particular ballot question.)

Original Report – Check this box if the report being filed is the initial report for this Reporting Period.

Amended Report – Check this box if the report being filed contains changes from the initial report for this Reporting Period.

Reporting Period Beginning Date – Enter the first date of the reporting period.

Reporting Period Ending Date – Enter the last date of the reporting period.

Name and Address of Contributor – Enter the name and address of the person contributing an amount in excess of one thousand eight hundred dollars ($1,800) per election cycle to a ballot question advocate for purposes of ballot question advocacy.

Place of Employment of Contributor, if Individual – Enter the name of the business at which the contributor is employed, provided the contributor is an individual.

Date Contribution Received – Enter the date that a donation in the form of money, gifts, loans, paid personal services, or contributions in-kind was received by the ballot question advocate.

Transaction Types – Acceptable entries for transaction types are:

Transaction Types	Description
• Cash	Contributions received by Cash from each person or source.
• Check	Contributions received by Check from each person or source.
• Money Order	Contributions received by Money Order from each person or source.
• Credit Card/Internet	Contributions received by Credit Card or through the Internet from each person or source.
• In-Kind	Non-monetary contribution of goods, services or other things of value received from each person or source.
• Other	Contributions received from other sources, i.e interest received, other receipts, refunds/rebates.

Amount of Contribution – Enter the amount contributed.

Page No. – Enter the specific page number and the total pages number of this "Schedule of Contributions for Ballot Question Advocacy" for this reporting period.

Page Total – Enter the sum of the contributions received as reported on this page, excluding in-kind contributions.

If you have any questions on how to complete this form, please contact the Board of Elections.

PENALTIES – Any person violating the provisions of the Rhode Island Ballot Advocacy and Reporting Act (Chapter 25.2 of Title 17 of the Rhode Island General Laws) shall be subject to penalties.

Please see reverse side for instructions on how to complete this form.

State of Rhode Island and Providence Plantations
Board of Elections
Campaign Finance Unit
50 Branch Avenue, Providence, Rhode Island 02904
Tel. (401) 222-2345
www.elections.ri.gov

SCHEDULE OF EXPENDITURES FOR BALLOT ADVOCACY (BQA-3)

Office Time Stamp

Full Name of Ballot Question Advocate

Reporting Period Beginning Date: _____

Reporting Period Ending Date: _____

☐ Original Report

☐ Amended Report

NAME AND ADDRESS OF PERSON TO WHOM EXPENDITURE WAS MADE	PURPOSE OF EXPENDITURE	DATE EXPENDITURE MADE	AMOUNT OF EXPENDITURE

PAGE NO: ____ OF ____

PAGE TOTAL $

BQA-3

07/05

INSTRUCTIONS

Full Name of Ballot Question Advocate – Enter the full name of the Ballot Question Advocate (Any person making an expenditure with a cumulative total that exceeds one thousand dollars ($1,000) in a calendar year for ballot question advocacy on a particular ballot question.)

Original Report – Check this box if the report being filed is the initial report for this Reporting Period.

Amended Report – Check this box if the report being filed contains changes from the initial report for this Reporting Period.

Reporting Period Beginning Date – Enter the first date of the reporting period.

Reporting Period Ending Date – Enter the last date of the reporting period.

Name and Address of Person To Whom Expenditure Was Made– Enter the name and address of the person or entity receiving an expenditure for ballot question advocacy , which in the aggregate exceeds one hundred dollars ($100).

Purpose of Expenditure – Enter a detailed description as to the reason for said expenditure.

Date Expenditure Was Made – Enter the date that a payment for any goods and services was made for the purpose of ballot question advocacy.

Amount of Expenditure – Enter the amount of money spent for the goods or services received for ballot question advocacy.

Page No. – Enter the specific page number and the total pages number of this *"Schedule of Contributions for Ballot Question Advocacy"* for this reporting period.

Page Total – Enter the sum of the contributions received as reported on this page

If you have any questions on how to complete this form, please contact the Board of Elections.

PENALTIES Any person violating the provisions of the Rhode Island Ballot Advocacy and Reporting Act (Chapter 25.2 of Title 17 of the Rhode Island General Laws) shall be subject to penalties.

177

State of Rhode Island and Providence Plantations
Board of Elections
Campaign Finance Unit
50 Branch Avenue, Providence, Rhode Island 02904
Tel. (401) 222-2345
www.elections.ri.gov

NOTICE OF ORGANIZATION (CF-1)

Time Stamp
(For Office Use Only)

Notice of Organization for:	Purpose:
☐ Candidate or Officeholder ☐ Political Party Committee ☐ Political Action Committee (PAC) *(Complete Back of Form)*	☐ Initial Notice of Organization ☐ Amendment to Notice of Organization ☐ Change of Treasurer or Deputy Treasurer ☐ Annual Political Party Treasurer's Filing

Full Name of Candidate, Officeholder, Political Party Committee, or Political Action Committee (PAC)　Key #

Street Address　City/Town, State and Zip Code

Mailing Address (if different)　City/Town, State and Zip Code

Telephone Number　Daytime Telephone Number　Fax Number　E-mail Address

If a Candidate, office being sought:

Party Affiliation, if any:　☐ Democratic　☐ Republican　☐ Other _____

APPOINTMENT/DESIGNATION OF TREASURER

As a Candidate, Officeholder or Chairperson of a Political Party or PAC named herein, I hereby:

☐ Designate as Treasurer　☐ Remove as Treasurer　☐ Designate as Deputy Treasurer　☐ Remove as Deputy Treasurer

the person named below, as required by law:

Name of Treasurer/Deputy Treasurer　Telephone Number　Daytime Telephone Number　Fax Number

Street Address　City/Town, State and Zip Code　E-mail Address

Mailing Address (if different)　City/Town, State and Zip Code

Subscribed and sworn before me this ___ day of _____ 20___.

X_____ Signature of Appointee　Date　X_____ Notary Public

APPOINTMENT/DESIGNATION OF TREASURER (If adding or removing more than one individual)

As a Candidate, Officeholder, or Chairperson of a Political Party or PAC named herein, I hereby:

☐ Designate as Treasurer　☐ Remove as Treasurer　☐ Designate as Deputy Treasurer　☐ Remove as Deputy Treasurer

the person named below, as required by law:

Name of Treasurer/Deputy Treasurer　Telephone Number　Daytime Telephone Number　Fax Number

Street Address　City/Town, State and Zip Code　E-mail Address

Mailing Address (if different)　City/Town, State and Zip Code

Subscribed and sworn before me this ___ day of _____ 20___.

X_____ Signature of Appointee　Date　X_____ Notary Public

Campaign Account Depositories:

Name(s) of Institution(s)	Number of Accounts (Example: One, Two)	Type of Account (Example: Checking, Savings)

Please attached additional sheets, if necessary

CF-1　**PLEASE COMPLETE BACK OF FORM**　Rev. 01/13

AFFIDAVIT

I, _____ , agree to abide by the
(Candidate, Officeholder, or Chairperson of Political Party Committee or PAC)

campaign finance laws of the State of Rhode Island and the rules and regulations ("rules") established by the Board of Elections ("Board") including, but not limited to, the prescribed manner and format for the reporting of all contributions and expenditures.

I hereby authorize the Treasurer/Deputy Treasurer appointed herein to act on my behalf and to perform all acts necessary to comply with the campaign finance laws of this state and the rules established by the Board and that the appointee's original signature indicates my specific authorization to act on my behalf.

I understand that I, and the Treasurer/Deputy Treasurer appointed herein, when issued a Personal Identification Number ("PIN") by the Board for the purpose of electronically filing reports and/or communications, that use of said PIN shall constitute my specific authorization to act on my behalf.

I understand that all communications by the Board to either myself or the Treasurer/Deputy Treasurer shall be directed to the mailing address(es) provided herein and that I am responsible for the receipt of all correspondence mailed to said address(es). Moreover, I understand that I am responsible for notifying the Board of any changes of address and that the failure to inform the Board of said change(s) shall not absolve me of my responsibilities under the law or rules of the Board.

I understand that I will be deemed to be the Treasurer if an amended "Notice of Organization" designating a new Treasurer is not received by the Board within ten (10) days of the death, resignation or removal of the Treasurer.

Notwithstanding the above, I acknowledge that I am ultimately solely and fully responsible for the activities of my campaign and/or committee including all reporting requirements and the payment of any and all fines assessed.

x_____
Signature of Candidate, Officeholder or   Date
Chairperson of Political Party or Political
Action Committee (PAC)

Subscribed and sworn before me this ___ day of _____ 20___.

X_____   X_____
Notary Public Signature   Notary Public (Print Name)

ADDITIONAL INFORMATION REQUIRED FROM POLITICAL ACTION COMMITTEE (PAC)

Name of Political Action Committee (PAC) Supporting or Opposing a Candidate (name as indicated on front of this form)

Name(s) and Address(es) of Officer(s) of Political Action Committee (PAC): (Attach additional list if necessary)

Name(s)	Title of Officer	Address	Telephone Number

Name(s) of any Candidate(s) whose election or defeat the Committee intends to advocate:

☐ Election   ☐ Defeat   _____
Name(s) of Candidate(s)

The membership and/or contributor base of the Political Action Committee is derived from the employees of one corporation or business entity or from one business or professional group or association or labor union.   ☐ Yes   ☐ No

If yes, identify the employer group, association or union: _____

Any report not completed properly will be returned and deemed not filed.
Only original signatures of candidates, treasurers and deputy treasurers need to be notarized.
If you have any questions on how to complete this form, please contact the Board of Elections.

PENALTIES: Any person violating the provisions of the Rhode Island Campaign Contributions and Expenditures Reporting Act (Chapter 25 of Title 17 of the Rhode Island General Laws) shall be subject to civil and/or criminal penalties.

Please see reverse side for instructions on how to complete this form.

State of Rhode Island and Providence Plantations
Board of Elections
Campaign Finance Unit
50 Branch Avenue, Providence, Rhode Island 02904
Telephone No. (401) 222-2345
www.elections.ri.gov

SUMMARY OF CAMPAIGN ACTIVITY (CF-2)

Time Stamp
(For Office Use Only)

Full Name of Candidate, Officeholder, Political Party Committee, or Political Action Committee (PAC)

Organization Key #

Street Address

City/Town, State and Zip Code

Mailing Address (if different)

City/Town, State and Zip Code

Telephone Number | Daytime Telephone Number | Fax Number | E-mail Address

Reporting Period (Dates):

Amended Report
Yes   No

Period Beginning: Period Ending:

Summary of Activity for Reporting Period

1. Beginning Cash Balance $
2. Cash Receipts
   a. Contributions From:
      1. Individuals $
      2. Political Parties $
      3. Political Action Committees $
      4. Loan Proceeds $
      5. Payroll Check Off (PAC's Only) $
   b. Other Receipts
      $
      $
      $
3. Total Cash Available (Add Lines 1 + 2a + 2b) $

4. Cash Disbursements
   a. Campaign Expenses $
   b. Repayment of Loans $
   c. Other Disbursements $
      $
      $
      $

5. Ending Cash Balance (Line 3 - 4a - 4b - 4c) $

6. Report of In-Kind Contributions $

Campaign Fund Status

Assets
7. Cash (Enter Amount from Line 5) $
8. Other Assets
      $
      $
      $
9. Total Assets (Add Lines 7 + 8) $

Liabilities and Fund Balance
10. Liabilities
   a. Accounts Payable $
   b. Loans Payable $
   c. Other Liabilities $
      $
      $
      $
11. Total Liabilities (Add Lines 10a+10b+10c) $

12. Total Fund Balance (Line 9 - Line 11) $

13. Total Funds Available (Line 5 - Line 11) $

I hereby certify that this report of campaign contributions and expenditures and the supporting documents are complete, true and correct.

Print Name of Person Completing Report

x
Signature of Person Completing Report   Date

Title of Person Completing Report

CF-2   Rev. 06/04

INSTRUCTIONS

The information reported is required under the Rhode Island Campaign Contributions and Expenditures Reporting Act of 1974 as amended.

Full Name of Candidate, Officeholder, Political Party Committee, or Political Action Committee (PAC) – Enter the full name of the candidate, officeholder, political party committee or political action committee as reported on the "Notice of Organization" (Form CF-1).

Organization Key # - Enter the unique number assigned to this organization by the Board of Elections.

Street Address – Enter the address of this organization as reported on the "Notice of Organization" (Form CF-1).

City/Town, State & Zip Code – Enter the City/Town, State and Zip Code as reported on the "Notice of Organization" (Form CF-1).

Mailing Address – Enter the address where mail is directed to this organization.

City/Town, State and Zip Code – Enter the City/Town, State and Zip Code where mail is directed to this organization.

Telephone Number – Enter the telephone number as reported on the "Notice of Organization (Form CF-1).

Daytime Telephone Number – Enter a secondary telephone for this organization.

Fax Number – Enter the fax number for this organization.

E-mail Address – Enter the E-mail address for this organization.

Reporting Period (Dates) – Enter the first date of the reporting period in the "Period Beginning" field and the last date of the reporting period in the "Period Ending" field. Note: Refer to the organization's "Reporting Schedule" for the beginning and ending reporting dates.

Amended Report – If this report is a correction of a previously filed report, circle "Yes", otherwise circle "No".

Beginning Cash Balance (Line 1)– Enter the amount of total cash (on hand and in the bank) this organization has as of the first date of the reporting period. NOTE: This amount should be the same amount as the Ending Cash Balance as reported on the organization's last filed report, if applicable.

Individuals (Line 2a1) – Enter the total amount of itemized and aggregated contributions received from individuals during this reporting period.

Political Parties (Line 2a2) - Enter the total amount of itemized and aggregated contributions received from Political Parties during this reporting period.

Political Action Committees (Line 2a3) - Enter the total amount of itemized and aggregated contributions received from Political Action Committees during this reporting period.

Loan Proceeds (Line 2a4) – Enter the total amount of funds loaned to this organization during this reporting period.

Payroll Check Off (Line 2a5) – Enter the total amount of funds received via Payroll Check Off during this reporting period. NOTE: This contribution type only applies to Political Action Committees (PACs).

Other Receipts (Line 2b) – Enter the total amount of funds received from sources other than those listed above. Ex: Interest Income, etc.

Total Cash Available (Line 3) – Add Lines 1, 2a, and 2b together and enter the amount on this line.

Campaign Expenses (Line 4a) – Enter the total amount of qualified itemized and aggregated campaign expenditures during this reporting period.

Repayment of Loans (Line 4b) – Enter the total amount of loans that were repaid during this reporting period.

Other Disbursements (Line 4c) - Enter the amount of funds spent for purposes other than those listed above.

Ending Cash Balance (Line 5) –Enter the total of (Line 3 – Line 4a - Line 4b - Line 4c).

Report of In-Kind Contributions (Line 6) – Enter the total of In-Kind Contributions received from individuals and committees.

Cash (Line 7) – Enter the total from Line 5.

Other Assets (Line 8) – List each asset other than cash and its monetary value on these lines.

Total Assets (Line 9) – Add Line 7 and Line 8 together and enter the amount.

Accounts Payable (Line 10a) – Enter the total amount owed by this organization but not yet paid.

Loans Payable (Line 10b) – Enter the total amount of funds previously recorded as "Loans Proceeds" that remain unpaid.

Other Liabilities (Line 10c) – Enter any other liabilities not listed on lines 10a or 10b.

Total Liabilities (Line 11) – Add Lines 10a, 10b and 10c together and enter the amount.

Total Fund Balance (Line 12) – Enter the total of (Line 9-Line 11).

Total Funds Available (Line 13) – Enter the total of (Line 5-Line 11).

Name/Title of Person Completing Report – This should be the treasurer, deputy treasurer, or the candidate, if his or her own treasurer.

REPORTS MUST BE SIGNED
Any report not completed or signed will be returned.
If you have any questions on how to complete this form, please contact the Board of Elections.

PENALTIES Any person violating the provisions of the Rhode Island Campaign Contributions and Expenditures Reporting Act (Chapter 25 of Title 17 of the Rhode Island General Laws) shall be subject to civil and/or criminal penalties.

Please see reverse side for instructions on how to complete this form.

State of Rhode Island and Providence Plantations
Board of Elections
Campaign Finance Unit
50 Branch Avenue, Providence, Rhode Island 02904
Tel. (401) 222-2345
www.elections.ri.gov

SCHEDULE OF CONTRIBUTIONS RECEIVED (CF-3)

Time Stamp
(For Office Use Only)

Key #	Full Name of Candidate, PAC or Party Committee	Amended Report		Reporting Period	
		Yes	No	From:	To:

Item #	Transaction Type Code (see back for list of codes)	Contribution Type Code (see back for list of codes)	Receipt Date	Deposit Date	Contribution Amount
					$

In-kind/Other Contribution Receipts Description:

Contributor Information					Employer Data	
Prefix	First Name	MI	Last Name or PAC/Party Committee Name	Suffix	Employer Name	
Street Address					Street Address	
City/Town			State	Zip Code	City/Town	State	Zip Code

Item #	Transaction Type Code (see back for list of codes)	Contribution Type Code (see back for list of codes)	Receipt Date	Deposit Date	Contribution Amount
					$

In-kind/Other Contribution Receipts Description:

Contributor Information					Employer Data	
Prefix	First Name	MI	Last Name or PAC/Party Committee Name	Suffix	Employer Name	
Street Address					Street Address	
City/Town			State	Zip Code	City/Town	State	Zip Code

Item #	Transaction Type Code (see back for list of codes)	Contribution Type Code (see back for list of codes)	Receipt Date	Deposit Date	Contribution Amount
					$

In-kind/Other Contribution Receipts Description:

Contributor Information					Employer Data	
Prefix	First Name	MI	Last Name or PAC/Party Committee Name	Suffix	Employer Name	
Street Address					Street Address	
City/Town			State	Zip Code	City/Town	State	Zip Code

Item #	Transaction Type Code (see back for list of codes)	Contribution Type Code (see back for list of codes)	Receipt Date	Deposit Date	Contribution Amount
					$

In-kind/Other Contribution Receipts Description:

Contributor Information					Employer Data	
Prefix	First Name	MI	Last Name or PAC/Party Committee Name	Suffix	Employer Name	
Street Address					Street Address	
City/Town			State	Zip Code	City/Town	State	Zip Code

PAGE NO: _____ OF _____

PAGE TOTAL $

CF-3

Rev. 04/04

INSTRUCTIONS

The information reported is required under the Rhode Island Campaign Contributions and Expenditures Reporting Act of 1974 as amended.

Key # – Enter the unique number assigned to this campaign by the Board of Elections.

Full Name of Candidate, Officeholder, Political Party Committee, or Political Action Committee (PAC) – Enter the full name of the candidate, officeholder, political party committee or political action committee as reported on the "Notice of Organization" (Form CF-1).

Amended Report – If this report is a correction of a previously filed report, circle "Yes", otherwise circle "No".

Reporting Period – Enter the first date of the reporting period in the "From" field and the last date of the reporting period in the "To" field. Note: Refer to the organization's "Reporting Schedule" for the beginning and ending reporting dates.

Item # - This is a sequential number the organization assigns to each transaction. For example, the first transaction is numbered 1, the second transaction is number 2, etc.

Transaction Type Code – Acceptable entries for the contribution transaction types are:

Transaction Type Code	Description
• Cash	$25 Cash limit from individuals, Political Action Committees (PACs), Political Party Committees.
• Check	Checks received from individuals, Political Action Committees (PACs), Political Party Committees.
• Money Order	Money Orders received from individuals, Political Action Committees (PACs), Political Party Committees.

Contribution Type Code – Acceptable entries for the contribution type are:

Contribution Type Code	Description
• Individual	Contribution received from an individual.
• Aggregate: (Individual, PAC, Party)	Contributions received are $100 or less per contributor per calendar year. Record a separate entry for each aggregate type (i.e. Aggregate (Individual); Aggregate (PAC); etc.)
• PAC (Political Action Committee)	Contribution received is from a Political Action Committee registered in Rhode Island.
• Party (Political Party Committee)	Contribution received is from a registered Political Party Committee.
• Loan Proceeds	Funds recorded with this contribution type code have to be repaid.
• In-Kind (Individual, PAC, Party)	Non-monetary value of goods or services received. Record a separate entry for each in-kind type (i.e. In-Kind (Individual); In-Kind (PAC); etc.)
• Interest Received	Interest received for having campaign funds in a federally insured depository.
• Refund/Rebate	Funds received as a result of a previous expenditure.
• Other Receipt	Funds received from a source other than those listed.

Receipt Date – The date the treasurer or deputy treasurer received the contribution.

Deposit Date – The date the treasurer or deputy treasurer deposited the contribution.

Contribution Amount – The amount of funds or value of the in-kind contribution received by the treasurer or deputy treasurer.

In-Kind/Other Contribution Receipts Description – Describe in detail the donated services received or a detailed description of the "Other Contribution Type" when selecting this option.

Contributor Name Prefix – Enter a name prefix as reported by the contributor. Example: Dr., Hon., Gen., etc.

Contributor First Name – Enter the first name of the contributor.

Contributor MI – Enter the middle initial of the contributor.

Contributor Last Name or PAC/Party Committee Name – Enter the last name of the contributor, or if a PAC or party, the name of the PAC or party as reported to the Board of Elections on its "Notice of Organization" (CF-1).

Contributor Suffix – Enter a name suffix as reported by the contributor. Example: Jr., III, Sr., etc.

Contributor Street Address – Enter the home address of the contributor.

Contributor City/Town, State, Zip Code – Enter the city or town, state and zip code of the contributor.

Contributor Employer Name – Enter the name of the business at which the contributor is employed.

Contributor Employer Address - Enter the address of the business at which the contributor is employed.

Contributor City/Town, State, Zip Code – Enter the city or town, state and zip code of the business at which the contributor is employed.

If you have any questions on how to complete this form, please contact the Board of Elections.

PENALTIES: Any person violating the provisions of the Rhode Island Campaign Contributions and Expenditures Reporting Act (Chapter 25 of Title 17 of the Rhode Island General Laws) shall be subject to civil and/or criminal penalties.

Please see reverse side for instructions on how to complete this form.

State of Rhode Island and Providence Plantations
Board of Elections
Campaign Finance Unit
50 Branch Avenue, Providence, Rhode Island 02904
Tel. (401) 222-2345
www.elections.ri.gov

SCHEDULE OF EXPENDITURES (CF-4)

Time Stamp
(For Office Use Only)

Key #	Full Name of Candidate, PAC or Party Committee	Amended Report	Reporting Period
		Yes No	From: To:

Check #	Expenditure Date	Payment Date	Disbursement Type (See back for list of codes)	Expenditure Type (See back for list of codes)	Expenditure Amount
					$

Purpose of Expenditure

Payee Information				
Prefix	First Name	MI Last Name or Vendor Name		Suffix
Street Address		City/Town	State	Zip Code

Check #	Expenditure Date	Payment Date	Disbursement Type (See back for list of codes)	Expenditure Type (See back for list of codes)	Expenditure Amount
					$

Purpose of Expenditure

Payee Information				
Prefix	First Name	MI Last Name or Vendor Name		Suffix
Street Address		City/Town	State	Zip Code

Check #	Expenditure Date	Payment Date	Disbursement Type (See back for list of codes)	Expenditure Type (See back for list of codes)	Expenditure Amount
					$

Purpose of Expenditure

Payee Information				
Prefix	First Name	MI Last Name or Vendor Name		Suffix
Street Address		City/Town	State	Zip Code

Check #	Expenditure Date	Payment Date	Disbursement Type (See back for list of codes)	Expenditure Type (See back for list of codes)	Expenditure Amount
					$

Purpose of Expenditure

Payee Information				
Prefix	First Name	MI Last Name or Vendor Name		Suffix
Street Address		City/Town	State	Zip Code

PAGE NO: _____ OF _____	PAGE TOTAL	$

CF-4   Rev. 04/04

INSTRUCTIONS

The information reported is required under the Rhode Island Campaign Contributions and Expenditures Reporting Act of 1974 as amended.

Key # – Enter the unique number assigned to this organization by the Board of Elections.

Full Name of Candidate, Officeholder, Political Party Committee, or Political Action Committee (PAC) – Enter the full name of the candidate, officeholder, political party committee or political action committee as reported on the "Notice of Organization" (Form CF-1).

Amended Report – If this report is a correction of a previously filed report, circle "Yes", otherwise circle "No".

Reporting Period – Enter the first date of the reporting period in the "From" field and the last date of the reporting period in the "To" field. Note: Refer to the organization's "Reporting Schedule" for the beginning and ending reporting dates.

Check # - Enter the organization's check number that was used to pay this expenditure.

Expenditure Date – Enter the date the expenditure was incurred (i.e. The date the organization received goods or services).

Payment Date – Enter the date the organization paid the expenditure for the goods or services received.

Disbursement Type – Acceptable entries for this field are:

Disbursement Type	Description
Campaign Expenditure	Any campaign expense paid for at the time of purchase.
Aggregate Expenditure	One or more expenses in which the total was $100 or less per payee within a calendar year.
Repayment of Loan	When a loan or portion of a loan is repaid.
Accounts Payable	When goods or services are received, but not paid. Example: Credit Card Purchases
Accounts Payable Repayment	Payment of expenditures that were previously reported as accounts payable. Example: Paid credit card bill.

Expenditure Type – Acceptable entries for this field are:

Expenditure Types
(Refer to the "Campaign Finance Manual" for descriptions and examples)

- Advertising
- Bank Fees
- Consultant & Professional Services
- Donations
- Employee Services
- Entertainment
- Food & Beverages
- Fundraising Expenses
- Gifts
- Legal & Accounting
- Meals
- Office Equipment
- Office Supplies
- Other
- Rent & Utilities
- Telephone

Expenditure Amount – Enter the amount of money spent on the goods or services received.

Purpose of Expenditure – Enter a detailed description as to the reason for said expense. Example: Lunch meeting at (Restaurant Name) to discuss pending legislation.

Payee Name Prefix – Enter the name prefix as reported by the payee. Example: Dr., Hon., Gen., etc.

Payee First Name – Enter the first name of the payee.

Payee MI – Enter the middle initial of the payee.

Payee Last Name or Vendor's Name – Enter the last name of the payee, or the vendor name.

Payee Suffix – Enter the name suffix as reported by the payee. Example: Jr., III, Sr., etc.

Payee Street Address – Enter the home address of the individual or the business address of the vendor.

Payee City/Town, State, Zip Code – Enter the city or town, state and zip code of the individual or vendor.

If you have any questions on how to complete this form, please contact the Board of Elections.

PENALTIES: Any person violating the provisions of the Rhode Island Campaign Contributions and Expenditures Reporting Act (Chapter 25 of Title 17 of the Rhode Island General Laws) shall be subject to civil and/or criminal penalties.

State of Rhode Island and Providence Plantations
Board of Elections
Campaign Finance Unit
50 Branch Avenue, Providence, Rhode Island 02904
Tel. (401) 222-2345
www.elections.ri.gov

AFFIDAVIT FOR ANNUAL FILING EXEMPTION (CF-5)

Time Stamp
(For Office Use Only)

Full Name of Candidate, Officeholder, Political Party Committee, or Political Action Committee (PAC)	Key #

Street Address	City/Town, State and Zip Code

Mailing Address (if different)	City/Town, State and Zip Code

Telephone Number	Daytime Telephone Number	Fax Number	E-mail Address

Report Year Requesting Exemption	Funds Available (See Instructions)	Accounts Payable (See Instructions)	Loans Payable (See Instructions)
	$	$	$

AFFIDAVIT

I, _____, do hereby certify in my capacity

Name of Treasurer

as treasurer, that I will accept no contributions in excess of $100 in the aggregate from a single source within this calendar year nor make aggregate expenditures in excess of $1,000 within this calendar year. *

X _____

Signature of Treasurer   **Date**

NOTES: If this affidavit is filed, the treasurer is excused from filing the periodic reports of contributions and expenditures. However, at the end of the calendar year, the campaign treasurer is required to file a "Summary of Campaign Activity" (CF-2), a "Schedule of Contributions Received" (CF-3) to report contributions, and a "Schedule of Expenditures" (CF-4) to report expenses.

Also, after executing this affidavit, a Candidate, Officeholder, PAC or Political Party Committee who in a calendar year accepts contributions in excess of $100 in the aggregate from a single source or incurs aggregate expenditures in excess of $1,000, the treasurer will immediately commence filing the required periodic reports.

INSTRUCTIONS

The information reported is required under the Rhode Island Campaign Contributions and Expenditures Reporting Act of 1974 as amended.

Full Name of Candidate, Officeholder, Political Party Committee, or Political Action Committee (PAC) – Enter the full name of the candidate, officeholder, political party committee or political action committee as reported on the "Notice of Organization" (Form CF-1).

Key # - Enter the unique number assigned to this organization by the Board of Elections.

Street Address – Enter the address of the organization as reported on the "Notice of Organization" (Form CF-1).

City/Town, State & Zip Code – Enter the city/town, state and zip code as reported on the "Notice of Organization" (Form CF-1).

Mailing Address – Enter the address where mail is directed to this organization.

City/Town, State and Zip Code – Enter the city/town, state and zip code where mail is directed to this organization.

Telephone Number – Enter the telephone number as reported on the "Notice of Organization" (Form CF-1).

Daytime Telephone Number – Enter a secondary telephone for this organization.

Fax Number – Enter the fax number for this organization.

E-mail Address – Enter the E-mail address for this organization.

Report Year Requesting Exemption – Enter the calendar year that the organization is requesting an annual exemption (Ex.: 2004).

Funds Available – Enter the total amount of money the organization has available as of January 1st of the report year (for ongoing organizations), or at the time of filing a declaration of candidacy (for new candidates), whichever is earlier.

Accounts Payable – Enter the total amount of money owed to others in exchange for goods and services already received as of January 1st of the report year, if applicable. This amount should match the accounts payable balance reported on the organization's last report filed with the Board of Elections.

Loans Payable – Enter the total amount of money owed by your organization that was previously recorded as "loan proceeds" as of January 1st of the report year, if applicable. This amount should match the Loans Payable balance on the last report filed with the Board of Elections.

If you have any questions on how to complete this form, please contact the Board of Elections.

PENALTIES: Any person violating the provisions of the Rhode Island Campaign Contributions and Expenditures Reporting Act (Chapter 25 of Title 17 of the Rhode Island General Laws) shall be subject to civil and/or criminal penalties.

CF-5   Rev. 04/04

State of Rhode Island and Providence Plantations
Board of Elections
Campaign Finance Unit
50 Branch Avenue, Providence, Rhode Island 02904
Tel. (401) 222-2345
www.elections.ri.gov

AFFIDAVIT DISSOLVING CAMPAIGN ACCOUNT (CF-7)

Time Stamp
(For Office Use Only)

Full Name of Candidate, Officeholder, Political Party Committee, or Political Action Committee (PAC)	Key #

Street Address	City/Town, State and Zip Code

Mailing Address (if different)	City/Town, State and Zip Code

Telephone Number	Daytime Telephone Number	Fax Number	E-mail Address

Campaign Dissolved as of (Date):

DECLARATION

Upon filing this form, there are no remaining campaign funds, and the organization (Candidate, Officeholder, Political Party, or Political Action Committee) has completed its business and is hereby dissolved.

AFFIDAVIT

I, _____, do hereby certify that the declaration provided above is true and correct.
_____Name of Treasurer_____

X_____
      Signature of Treasurer   **Date**

INSTRUCTIONS

The information reported is required under the Rhode Island Campaign Contributions and Expenditures Reporting Act of 1974 as amended.

Full Name of Candidate, Officeholder, Political Party Committee, or Political Action Committee (PAC) – Enter the full name of the candidate, officeholder, political party committee or political action committee as reported on the "Notice of Organization" (Form CF-1).

Key # - Enter the unique number assigned to this campaign by the Board of Elections.

Street Address – Enter the address of this organization as reported on the "Notice of Organization" (Form CF-1).

City/Town, State & Zip Code – Enter the city/town, state and zip code as reported on the "Notice of Organization" (Form CF-1).

Mailing Address – Enter the address where mail is directed to this organization.

City/Town, State and Zip Code – Enter the city/town, state and zip code where mail is directed to this organization.

Telephone Number – Enter the telephone number as reported on the "Notice of Organization" (Form CF-1).

Daytime Telephone Number – Enter a secondary telephone for this campaign.

Fax Number – Enter the fax number for this campaign.

E-mail Address – Enter the E-mail address for this campaign.

Campaign Dissolved as of (Date) – Enter the date the campaign has concluded its business.

If you have any questions on how to complete this form, please contact the Board of Elections.

PENALTIES   Any person violating the provisions of the Rhode Island Campaign Contributions and Expenditures Reporting Act (Chapter 25 of Title 17 of the Rhode Island General Laws) shall be subject to civil and/or criminal penalties.

CF-7   Rev. 05/04

State of Rhode Island and Providence Plantations
Board of Elections
Campaign Finance Division
50 Branch Avenue, Providence, Rhode Island 02904
Tel. (401) 222-2345
www.elections.ri.gov

REPORT OF INDEPENDENT EXPENDITURES, ELECTIONEERING COMMUNICATIONS OR COVERED TRANSFERS (CF-8)

Time Stamp
(Office Use Only)

Identify Person, Business Entity or PAC responsible for Independent Expenditure, Electioneering Communication or Covered Transfer

Street Address	City/Town, State and Zip Code	Telephone Number
Employer (if applicable)	Occupation (if applicable)	

The Person, Business Entity or PAC has expended more than $1000 to support or defeat a Candidate or Referendum as follows:

Identify the Candidate(s) on the ballot and whether funds were expended to support or defeat this candidate

_____: ☐ Support ☐ Defeat

Identify the Referendum on the ballot and whether funds where expended to support or defeat this referendum

_____: ☐ Support ☐ Defeat

Any person, business entity or political action committee making independent expenditures, electioneering communications, or covered transfers shall report all such expenditures provided the total of the money so expended exceeds $1000 within a calendar year to the Board of Elections within 7 days of making the expenditure.

Date of Expenditure	Amount of Expenditure	EXPENDITURES Name and Full Address: Person, Business Entity, PAC Receiving Expenditure
	$	
	$	
	$	
	$	
	$	

Year to Date Total of All Expenditures in Support or Defeat of This Candidate or Referendum: $

Reports of independent expenditures, electioneering communications or covered transfers by a person, business entity or PAC shall disclose the identity of all donors of an aggregate of $1000 or more within the current election cycle.

Date Donation Received	Donation Amount	DONATIONS Name, Address and Place of Employment of Donor
	$	
	$	
	$	
	$	
	$	

Amount from Person's, Business Entity's or PAC's own funds for independent expenditures, electioneering communications or covered transfers in Support or Defeat of this Candidate or Referendum: $

< Please Sign on Reverse Side >

188

The person named below affirms, under penalty of false statement, that no expenditure contained herein is coordinated with the candidate or referendum whose support or defeat is promoted and that information provided is true and accurate and complies with RI General Laws and with Rules and Regulations adopted pursuant to RIGL §17-25.3 et seq.

Identification of Person Responsible for Making Expenditure	
Signature of Person Responsible for Making Expenditure	Subscribed and Sworn to me this _____ Date
Address, City/Town, State, Zip Code of Person Making Expenditure	x_____ Notary Public

Reporting Requirements for Independent Expenditures, Electioneering Communications and Covered Transfers

WHO NEEDS TO FILE:
It is lawful for any person, business entity or political action committee (PAC), not otherwise prohibited by law and not acting in coordination with a candidate, authorized candidate committee, PAC or political party committee, to expend personally from that person's own funds a sum which is not to be repaid for any purpose not prohibited by law to support or defeat a candidate or referendum.

WHEN TO FILE:
Any person, business entity or PAC making independent expenditures, electioneering communications or covered transfers shall report all such expenditures, provided the total of the money so expended exceeds $1000 within a calendar year, to the Board of Elections within seven (7) days of making the expenditure.

After a person, business entity or PAC files its initial report, the person, business entity or PAC shall file an additional report after each time the person, business entity or PAC makes or contracts to make independent expenditures, electioneering communications or covered transfers aggregating an additional $1,000 with respect to the same election as that which the initial report relates.

When a report is required within thirty (30) days prior to the election to which the expenditure was directed, it shall be filed within twenty-four (24) hours of the expenditure. When such a report is required at any other time, it shall be filed within seven (7) days after the expenditure.

WHAT TO FILE:
Reports of independent expenditures, electioneering communications or covered transfers by a person shall contain the name, street address, city, state, zip code, occupation, employer, of the person responsible for the expenditure, the name street address, city, state, zip code of the person receiving the expenditure, the date and amount of each expenditure and the year-to-date total. The report shall also include a statement identifying the candidate or referendum that the independent expenditure or electioneering communication is intended to promote the success or defeat, and affirm under penalty of false statement that the expenditure is not coordinated with the candidate or referendum in question.

Reports shall also disclose the identify, which includes the name, address and place of employment and donation amount, of all donors of an aggregate of $1000 or more to such person, business entity or PAC within the current election cycle.

PENALTIES:
Any person, who willfully and knowingly violates the provisions of Chapter 25.3 of Title 17 shall, upon conviction, be guilty of a misdemeanor and shall be fined not more than $1000 per violation. The state Board of Elections may impose a civil penalty upon any person, business or PAC who violates the provisions of Chapter 25.3 of Title 17 in the amount of $1000, or up to 150% of the aggregate amount of the independent expenditures, electioneering communications or covered transfers per violation, whichever is greater.

THIS FORM MUST BE RETURNED TO THE BOARD OF ELECTIONS BEARING ORIGINAL SIGNATURES.

If you have any questions on how to complete this form, please contact the Board of Elections.

CF-8   Rev. 09/12

Declaration of Candidacy Form

State of Rhode Island and Providence Plantations
DECLARATION OF CANDIDACY

Federal and Statewide Offices to be filed with the Office of the Secretary of State, and
State and Local Offices to be filed with the Local Board of Canvassers during the period from

JUNE 23, 2014 TO JUNE 25, 2014 NOT LATER THAN 4 P.M.

The undersigned hereby declares that he or she is eligible under the provisions of Chapter 17-14 of the General Laws of 1956, as amended, in the case of party candidates, to be a candidate to be voted for at a Primary to be held on September 9, 2014, or in the case of unaffiliated candidates to be a candidate at the General Election to be held on November 4, 2014 and makes the following declarations:

NAME OF CANDIDATE AND ADDRESS: As they appear on the voting list (PRINT OR TYPE)

Name of Candidate

Address   City or Town   State   Zip

FILING DECLARATION AS: (CHECK ONLY ONE)

Declaration for Party Candidate: OR   **Declaration for Independent/Unaffiliated Candidate:**

- [ ] Democrat
- [ ] Moderate
- [ ] Republican
- [ ] Non-Partisan Local Office

- [ ] Independent
- [ ] Other _____

Indicate Organization/Political Principle represented - Cannot be more than 3 words and cannot contain the words "Democrat", "Moderate" or "Republican".

TITLE OF OFFICE: (CHECK ONLY ONE OFFICE ON THIS FORM AND ENTER DISTRICT NUMBER IF APPLICABLE)

Federal: [ ] Senator in Congress   [ ] Representative in Congress - Congressional District ____

Statewide: [ ] Governor   [ ] Lt. Governor   [ ] Secretary of State   [ ] Attorney General   [ ] General Treasurer

State: [ ] Senator in General Assembly - District ____   [ ] Representative in General Assembly - District ____

     [ ] Senatorial District Committee - District ____   [ ] Representative District Committee - District ____

     [ ] Democratic State Committeeman - District ____   [ ] Democratic State Committeewoman - District ____

Local Office: [ ] _____ Ward/District (if applicable) ____
        Title of local office being sought

PROVIDE THE FOLLOWING INFORMATION: Phone Number _____

Date of Birth   Place of Birth (Indicate City or Town, and State)

Length of Residence in Rhode Island   Length of Residence in City or Town

I hereby certify that I am not now imprisoned upon a felony conviction, nor have I been lawfully adjudicated to be non compos mentis (of unsound mind); and (if a party candidate) I have not been a member of a political party other than the declared party within ninety (90) days of filing date.

If a candidate for state or local public office, I hereby certify that I have not within the preceding three (3) years served any sentence, incarcerated or suspended, on probation or parole, for a crime committed after November 5, 1986 upon a plea of nolo contendere or guilty or upon a conviction for a felony or for a misdemeanor for which a sentence of imprisonment for six (6) months or more, whether suspended or to be served was imposed.

By signing and filing this declaration of candidacy, it is my express intention to withdraw any and all declarations of candidacy that I previously filed for any state or local public office during this current declaration period. I do so with full knowledge that any previously filed declaration of candidacy shall become null and void.

WITNESSES: Signature of Candidate as it appears on voting list

     Signature   Residence

     Signature   Residence

E-20E 2014

Paul F. Caranci

Sample Endorsement by Party Committee Form

STATE OF RHODE ISLAND AND PROVIDENCE PLANTATIONS
Office of the Secretary of State
To be filed with Local Board of Canvassers not later than
July 1, 2010 at 4 p.m.*
ENDORSEMENT BY PARTY COMMITTEE

Board of Canvassers
City or Town Hall

_____, Rhode Island
(City or Town)

Dear Sir or Madam:

Acting under and by virtue of the authority conferred by Title 17 of the General Laws of 1956, as amended, the undersigned are hereby directed to notify you that the following committee:

Check Party:	Check One:	For District Number:	For the City or Town of:
☐ Democrat	☐ Senatorial District Committee		
☐ Moderate	☐ Representative District Committee		
☐ Republican	☐ Ward Committee	(complete if a district or ward committee)	(complete if a city or town committee)
	☐ City or Town Committee		

at a meeting held on _____ endorsed the following as
(Date of Meeting)

its candidate(s) to be voted for at the primary to be held on September 14, 2010.

NAME OF CANDIDATE(S) (as it appears on declaration)	RESIDENCE (Street and Number)	TITLE OF OFFICE AND DISTRICT
1.		
2.		
3.		
4.		
5.		
6.		
7.		
8.		
9.		

* Senatorial and Representative District Committees in Providence must file with Secretary of State, Elections Division, 148 W. River St. Providence.

Party	Name of Committee	City, Town or District
	Signature	Title
	Signature	Title

Voting Precinct 1A

Bingo Sheet

7 a.m. to 8 a.m.

A	B	C	D	E	F	G
H	I	J	K	L	M	N
O	P	O	R	S	T	U
V	W	X	Y	Z		

Signature of Poll Bingo Worker

Glossary of Terms

Aggregate Campaign Contributions – the total campaign contributions made by one donor during an entire campaign cycle. (Chapter 6)

Bingo System – a system designed to identify and track campaign supporters (as well as supporters of your opponents) for purpose of ensuring that a greater number of your supporters participate in, and vote, in the election. (Chapters 10, 11 and 12)

Brochure – a "political resume" of sorts that includes a candidate biography, platform, education summary, organizational involvement and other relevant and related activities. It is an essential part of the message delivery system. (Chapter 7)

Campaign Contributions – the donation to your political campaign made by an individual, PAC or other allowable donor. (Chapter 6)

Campaign Finance Reporting Forms – the various forms (several depending upon political jurisdiction) required of candidates who are running for office and/or raising campaign funds. (Chapter 6)

Declaration of Candidacy – the process of formally declaring your candidacy for a specific office and under a particular party label. (Chapters 2 and 6)

Declaration Period – a set of days in which every person desirous of running for an elective office must file with the appropriate authority a declaration of candidacy. (Chapters 2 and 6)

Get Out the Vote (GOTV) – the collective activities throughout the campaign that identify your voters and ensure that those identified actually cast ballots in the campaign.

Hatch Act – A federal law that prohibits certain employees from fundraising or campaigning for certain public offices. (Chapter 5)

Illegal Contribution – one that is prohibited by the federal or state constitutions and laws as well as any federal, state or local rules and regulations *(see also prohibited contribution.* (Chapter 6)

Incumbent – a person who is serving in an elected position. (Chapters 2 and 3)

Leaflet – a detailed description of one or two platform planks. Generally much shorter yet much more detailed than the brochure, it is an alternate form of message delivery. (Chapter 7)

Message – defines the reasons that you are running for office. (Chapter 6)

Message Delivery – the vehicles that will be used to deliver your campaign message to the voters during the election cycle.

Name Recognition – a term that refers to the number of voters in your district that are familiar with your name prior to, or will become familiar with your name during, the election.

Nomination Papers – the official papers provided by the local elections board on which a prospective candidate must gather signatures allowing his/her name to appear on a ballot. (Chapter 6)

Nomination Period – the period of time in which a prospective candidate must gather a sufficient number of qualified signatures allowing his/her name to appear on a ballot. (Chapters 2 and 6)

Open Seat – an elected position in which no incumbent is running for re-election. (Chapter 3)

PAC – a group that raises money and donates to political causes or candidates *(see also political action committee.)* (Chapter 6)

Plank – an individual issue that you will address in your campaign. (Chapter 4)

Platform – the collective issues (planks) being addressed in your campaign. (Chapter 4)

Political Action Committee (PAC) - a group that raises money and donates to political causes or candidates *(see also PAC.)* (Chapter 6)

Political Strategy – the approach you will take to win the election. (Chapter 6)

Press Release – a document that is intended to inform the media of a proposal, an event or some other element of your campaign that you want to circulate to the general public. (Chapters 9 and 10)

Prohibited Contribution – one that is prohibited by the federal or state constitutions and laws as well as any federal, state or local rules and regulations *(see also illegal contribution.)* (Chapter 6)

Qualified Elector – a person who meets all the requirements that enable him/her to cast an election ballot in a specific voting precinct. (Chapter 2)

Qualified Signature – a signature from a qualified elector typically collected on the nomination papers that permit a candidate's name to appear on the ballot. (Chapter 6)

Single Issue Candidate – a candidate who's platform contains only a single plank. (Chapter 4)

Walking Sheets – a system of tracking and ranking voters during routine campaign activities. The walking sheets form the basis of the bingo system. (Chapters 6, 7, 10, 11 and12)

About the Author

Paul F. Caranci was appointed Deputy Secretary of State in 2007 and still serves in that capacity. He worked on his first presidential campaign in 1968, passing out leaflets for Richard Nixon and has worked on local, state or national campaigns almost every year since. In 1986 he was appointed to serve on the North Providence Zoning Board of Review and served in that position until he was elected to the North Providence Town Council in 1994 where he served for almost 17 years rising to the level of Vice-President.

He was also elected to many positions within the Democrat Party including the Representative District Committee, the Rhode Island Democratic State Committee, where he was appointed to the organization's Executive Committee, and the North Providence Democrat Town Committee where he served for almost 20 years also rising to the position of Vice-President.

During his tenure on the town council Paul was responsible for enacting such programs as bicycle police patrols in the town's six villages, community policing, curbside recycling, historic district zoning, and the creation of special zones for adult-entertainment facilities that prevented their location near residential zones or in places where children congregate. He also increased fines for the illegal sale of tobacco products to minors, created a land-trust for the preservation of open-space, passed an ordinance authorizing the recording and airing of all council meetings on cable television and developed alternate budget proposals intended to hold the line on taxes. He passed an ordinance prohibiting the use of eminent domain for commercial purposes and He collaborated with other council members to draft and pass a local ethics ordinance. His undercover work with the FBI exposed municipal corruption that led to the arrest, conviction and imprisonment of three sitting councilmen, including the council president, a former town council president, a former town solicitor and a strip club manager that acted as a middleman in the council's illegal bribery and kickback scheme. In addition, Paul co-authored reports that led to ethics charges and financial penalties against a zoning board member, forcing his resignation and an acting finance director forcing her removal from the position. An unlicensed insurance broker and a radio DJ were also convicted of federal charges as a result of their part in the criminal activities.

These actions and many other proposals that Paul championed helped to improve the quality of life for all residents of a town that his family has called home for five generations.

Paul is married to his childhood sweetheart Margie, and the couple has two adult children, Heather and Matthew and four grandsons, Matthew Jr., Jacob, Vincent and Casey. This is his fifth book.

Photo Credits

Chapter 1: "The age of brass. or the triumphs of Woman's rights", an 1869 lithograph print published by Currier and Ives. United States Library of Congress's Prints and Photographs division under the digital ID cph.3a04616

Chapter 2: "Durham County Board of Elections Office," 2008 by Ildar Sagdejev. This file is licensed under the Creative Commons Attribution 2.0 Generic license.

Chapter 3: "Pic of campaign signs in Apex, North Carolina," by Seth Ilys. This image is in the public domain.

Chapter 4: "Skeletons in the Closet," 2007, Thinkstock.

Chapter 5: " Working America Field Manager Dave Ninehouser at a Working America member's door," 2008 Molly Theobald This file is licensed under the Creative Commons Attribution 2.0 Generic license.

Chapter 6: "Campaign Supporters with candidate placards outside the Ward 1 polling station in Nashua, New Hampshire." This file is made available under the Creative Commons CC0 1.0 Universal Public Domain Dedication.

Chapter 7: "Icon of U.S. Currency," *This work is in the **public domain** in the United States under the terms of* Title 17, Chapter 1, Section 105 of theUS Code.

Chapter 8: " Sestak for Senate Campaign Office, Scranton, PA" This file is licensed under the Creative Commons Attribution 2.0 Generic license.

Chapter 9: " :Jack Kemp as he leaves a meet-the-candidates rally for 1988 Republican presidential candidates at county stadium in Union, SC on October 3, 1987," by Ray Gronberg. This file is licensed under the Creative Commons Attribution 2.0 Generic license.

Chapter 10: "Paul F. Caranci at the Rhode Island State House," from the collection of Paul F. Caranci.

Chapter 11: " Black and white bingo card," by Abbey Hendrickson. This file is licensed under the Creative Commons Attribution 2.0 Generic license.

Chapter 12: "2008 LA CA Democratic Primary ballot." This work is in the **public domain** pursuant to court interpretation of the Sunshine Amendment of the Constitution of California, and/or the California Public Records Act (CPRA), which contained no relevant provision(s) for copyright.

Chapter 13: " Early voting center at Bauer Drive Community Recreation Center in Rockville, Maryland, 2012," by Ben Schumin. This file is licensed under the Creative Commons Attribution 2.0 Generic License.

Chapter 14: "Super Tuesday Vote Utah," by Brian of Bountiful, Utah, 2008. This file is licensed under the Creative Commons Attribution 2.0 Generic License.

Chapter 15: "EPP Election Night, 2014. This file is licensed under the Creative Commons Attribution 2.0 Generic License.

Chapter 16: "3D Judge's Gavel," by Chris Potter, 2012. This file is licensed under the Creative Commons Attribution 2.0 Generic License.

Conclusion: "Women's Suffrage headquarters Cleveland , 1911," Library of Congress. This image is in the public domain.

Back Cover: "Paul F. Caranci at the Jimmy Carter Library, Plains, GA, 2014. From the collection of Paul F. Caranci.

Made in the USA
San Bernardino, CA
08 February 2017